PRACTICAL
HOUSE
PLANT BOOK

PRACTICAL
HOUSE
PLANT BOOK

FRAN BAILEY
ZIA ALLAWAY

CONTENTS

INTRODUCTION

Science has proved it: houseplants make us happier and healthier. When studies tell us that plants can purify the air, lift our mood, and reduce our stress levels, we have every reason to fill our homes with wonderful, happiness-inducing plants of every shape, size, and color.

With so many different varieties offered, there is a plant—or twenty—to suit everyone: elegant, blossoming orchids; tiny little cacti and succulents; delicate trailing plants; floor-standing palms and foliage plants … the list goes on and on. It's hard to resist the urge to simply fill any and every available surface with a random assortment of greenery, but the best houseplant displays are those that go one step further: thoughtful, curated arrangements that can create a mood within a home, be it a cosy little oasis or a dramatic, architectural plant display.

As much as we may want to, we can't all turn our homes into a full-scale botanical garden. Instead, we need to be a little more inventive. Poor light? Look for unfussy foliage plants, such as cast iron plants or snake plants, that can survive in a shadier spot. No free surface space? Plant up a miniature garden inside a glass terrarium, or go all out and create a hanging garden with macramé planters and kokedama.

And, once you've designed your plant-filled home, how exactly do you keep the plants in peak condition? With this book, you'll be able to care for whichever plants you choose, keep them healthy and strong, and take cuttings to share with friends and family (or to grow your own collection). Treat your plants well and, no matter how large or small your collection, you'll be rewarded with an indoor garden you can enjoy for years to come.

DESIGNING WITH HOUSEPLANTS

THE ART OF
HOUSEPLANT DESIGN

On its own, a plant is just a plant. Add another and it becomes a display. But what distinguishes a random selection of plants from a piece of design that can engage the eye and evoke the mood of your living space? The answer is to establish a visual connection between your plants using the four design elements below.

SCALE pp.14–17

Use size and proportion to create a display. Choose same-sized plants for balance and symmetry, or use plants of different sizes to draw the eye and create flow and movement.

SHAPE pp.18–21

Choosing plants with similar shapes can create beautiful, natural patterns, while contrasting shapes can be used to sculpt displays with a sense of drama.

"Think of your design from every angle, as if it is a three-dimensional piece of living sculpture."

COLOR pp.22-25

Color interacts with color in a way that color in isolation does not. Use that interplay to find soft, harmonious shades or build a more energetic, contrasting palette.

TEXTURE pp.26-29

A plant's texture can have visual as well as tactile appeal, as it determines how the foliage interacts with the light. Mix and match different textures to add depth to a display.

THE RULES OF
HOUSEPLANT DESIGN

How you choose to design your houseplant collection depends on your personal style, imagination, and the living space you have available. With so many variables, the possibilities are almost endless. But for your displays to be successful, follow these key principles.

1 CARE COMES BEFORE STYLE

A healthy plant is a beautiful plant. When designing for a particular space, always choose plants that you know will thrive in the light, temperature, and humidity conditions provided by that space. There is no point in taking the time to arrange the perfect display, only to watch the plants within it begin to wilt and die because they are unhappy in their location.

2 THINK NATURAL

Be inspired by nature. Consider where and how a plant would grow in the wild, and try to emulate that in your display. So if a plant thrives on a damp, semishaded forest floor, provide it with a position that offers a similar environment. If it trails from high branches, place it in a hanging container. If it grows aerial roots without soil, build that into your display. Whatever its natural circumstances, use them as inspiration.

3 HARMONY AND CONTRAST

Strike a balance between harmonious and contrasting design features. Familiarize yourself with the four key elements of design (see pp.10–11), and harmonize or contrast them as needed to achieve the effect you want. Harmony can create a balanced, unified appearance, while contrast will add interest and dynamism to a display.

UNDERSTANDING
SCALE

To put it simply, scale refers to the relative size and proportion of objects. A plant may be large or small, but its relationship with neighboring plants or objects is what defines its scale. Proportion is key to any successful design: a tiny cactus and a weeping fig, for example, would be totally out of scale and proportion with each other. Get the scale right, and you can create interesting relationships between the plants in your display.

HARMONY OF SCALE

Choosing and grouping together plants of uniform or nearly uniform scale results in a classic, highly ordered display. Repetition of scale and proportion creates a harmonious pattern and offers a sense of unity and simplicity. Harmony can become dull if the repetition is overdone, but in moderation it offers a sense of order and rhythm.

WHAT IS SCALE?

Scale describes your plants' sizes in comparison with one another. It is closely related to proportion, which describes the size of your plants within an overall display. Plants of a similar size are harmonious in scale, while those of different heights contrast in scale. Scale is relative: any two plants can share the same contrast of scale, provided that they maintain the same proportions.

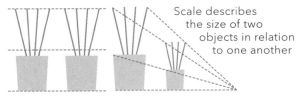

Scale describes the size of two objects in relation to one another

Harmony of scale   *Contrast of scale*

Fiddle-leaf figs

"How do your houseplants measure up against one another?"

CONTRAST OF SCALE

When plants are in proportion but of different scales, the eye is led from one to the other and the relationship is less static, and more dynamic, than that of a harmonious display. There is a sense of movement, going from small up to large, drawing the eye to a focal point in the grouping but maintaining proportion so that the relationship isn't broken.

Golden ball cacti

DESIGNING WITH HARMONY OF SCALE

Harmony can reinforce pattern, so use plants of the same scale to echo and exaggerate existing patterns within your living space, such as the symmetry of a windowsill or the staggered surface of a flight of stairs. Maintaining the same scale across a display while varying other design elements creates a harmonious pattern that unites your plants.

1 The uniform scale of these three kentia palms allows the display to echo the outline of the steps.

2 This cluster of three very different trailing plants is given cohesion by its harmony of scale (left to right: donkey's tail, string of pearls, and mistletoe cactus).

"Keep the scale of your plant display in proportion with your space to create equilibrium."

DESIGNING WITH
SCALE

What effect do you wish to create in your space? Do you want a formal pattern of repetition and harmony, or an informal, eye-catching arrangement that creates contrast and movement? You can lead the eye up or down, screen or define a space, or instantly introduce formality or informality simply with the proportion of your plant choices.

DESIGNING WITH CONTRAST OF SCALE

Grouping plants of different sizes offers a chance to manipulate the eye and generate a sense of movement. Perhaps you want to sweep along a windowsill or table, or conjure an impression of height, or lead the eye into a particular space. Use contrast of scale to create a sight line between your plants and draw attention to a focal point within your grouping.

1 A sequence of ever-larger bromeliads creates a line of visual interest along a windowsill, with a smaller one at the end just to playfully challenge the order.

2 The extreme contrast of scale between the little missionary plant and the imposing Swiss cheese plant is given cohesion by the midsized fiddle-leaf fig, which unifies and balances the display.

UNDERSTANDING
SHAPE

While every plant has its own particular growth habit, most will conform to a range of shapes that you can use to sculpt an overall line or outline for your display. Depending on how you arrange them, you can create a variety of effects, from a dynamic sweep to an ordered, symmetrical pattern.

WHAT IS SHAPE?

Every houseplant is unique, shaped as much by its environment as by its natural form, and no two plants will ever share an identical outline. Nevertheless, certain shapes tend to occur regularly throughout a range of houseplant types. Use these as a starting point when identifying your plant's outline.

Tall, architectural, jagged

Rosette-shaped

Domed, round

Trailing

Unstructured, wild

HARMONY OF SHAPE

A row of the same plant varieties, or of plants that have a similar shape, creates a harmonious pattern. The repetition of shape provides a sense of order and symmetry. No one plant may dominate, so the overall effect is of unity and simplicity, with all plants in the group having a similar visual weight.

Tall, architectural pencil cactus

CONTRAST OF SHAPE

Using a variety of shapes creates a sense of movement and draws the attention along the display. Diverse shapes can be used to create a sense of adventure and tension, with the visual weight being carried across the group according to how the shapes of the different plants interact.

Tall, architectural variegated snake plant

Tall, architectural aloe vera

Trailing mistletoe cactus

"Reposition your plants a few times until you're happy that they create a natural, flowing movement within the display."

DESIGNING WITH
SHAPE

Use the shapes of your plants to construct and sculpt a display that offers real visual impact in your living space. Establish patterns by repeating one or two strong shape types, or sculpt a unique outline from plants with distinct forms that will carry the eye through the design. To keep your displays controlled, prune them back regularly into shape (see pp.194–95).

DESIGNING WITH HARMONY OF SHAPE

Repetition of shape across a symmetrical design creates a sense of impact and order. Use plants with strong, clean outlines, such as tall or domed shapes, and limit the display to just one or two plant varieties to establish a sense of order and control.

1

2

1 These variegated snake plants and aloes share the same tall, architectural shape, creating a strong, symmetrical display.

2 Despite contrast of color, the matching forms of these begonias unify the display.

3 The repeated domes of baby's tears plants draw the eye along the table.

DESIGNING WITH CONTRAST OF SHAPE

An asymmetrical display built from multiple shape types can be used to redefine a space. Use different plants' unique visual features to create a flowing, organic design, but keep it controlled; the outline should lead the eye across the display without any obvious, irregular gaps that could break the flow.

1 The central cluster of mini succulents nestled within the larger trio builds into a varied but strongly united grouping.

2 The contrasting forms of the tall Swiss cheese plant and trailing golden pothos create a flowing, asymmetrical design bound together by the midsized plants in the group.

1

3

2

UNDERSTANDING COLOR

Within Nature there are many different colors, shades, and tones for you to work with. Colors have emotional properties, too: greens, the predominant color of plant design, are restful and reassuring; reds and oranges suggest warmth and energy; white evokes purity and calm. Use them to set the mood for your space.

HARMONY OF COLOR

Restricting your palette to different shades of the same color creates a sense of order and control. Limiting an arrangement to such a narrow section of the color wheel can also provide an air of calm and tranquility. Mixing in colors that lie adjacent on the color wheel, such as soft blues or gentle yellows, changes the rhythm but doesn't unbalance the overall equilibrium. The colors still harmonize and blend with each other, maintaining the simplicity.

WHAT IS COLOR?

Colors in isolation behave differently from colors in combination, and the color wheel shows how those relationships work. In between the primary colors of red, blue, and yellow lie all the shades they make in combination (so, for example, green sits between blue and yellow, which combine to make green). Toward the center are progressively lighter tints, while as the circle progresses outward, the shades get darker.

The color wheel shows all colors, along with their hues, tints, tones, and shades.

Adjacent colors work in harmony, as they share the same range of hues and tones.

Opposing colors on the wheel can create contrast and vibrancy.

yellow-greens   *blue-greens*   *blue-purples*

CONTRAST OF COLOR

Using colors from opposite sides of the color wheel, such as red and green or yellow and purple, instantly adds energy to a display. For a more subtle effect, try working with three colors evenly spaced around the color wheel (green, orange, and purple, for instance); while still contrasting, the palette is not as high-energy as a two-color, directly opposing contrast would be.

"Nature offers a wonderful variety of colors from which you can create your own artist's palette."

DESIGNING WITH
COLOR

Color evokes emotion, so design your display according to the mood you want to create. For a sense of serenity, try greens and whites; for a vibrant display, incorporate fiery oranges and reds. Cool colors can also impart a sense of space, while warm colors may suggest cosiness.

DESIGNING WITH HARMONY OF COLOR

For a calm, ordered arrangement, plants need to blend gently with one another color-wise. A strict color palette of greens is refined, but you may need to vary other elements to avoid a dull display. Broadening your palette to adjacent colors allows a wider range of moods to be conjured, while retaining serenity and order. Cool hues generally suggest a sense of space.

1 A palette of purple flowers and foliage harmonizes this group of different plants, setting a gentle yet welcoming mood.

2 This little succulent display creates a muted range of greens, from the red-green *Kalanchoe* to the white-speckled haworthia.

3 The rattlesnake plant's variegated green leaves (left) offer some interest when paired with the fiddle-leaf fig behind it.

"Color is a powerful tool for influencing the senses and creating a particular atmosphere or mood."

1

2

3

DESIGNING WITH CONTRAST OF COLOR

Warm colors can make spaces appear more intimate. As they contrast directly with green, they also add drama to a plant display. Use them to draw the eye in to your display, or to create bold, vibrant relationships between your plants.

1 The vivid orange moth orchid picks up on the terracotta pots and stands out as the focal point in the display.

2 Make an air plant display pop with a few red-colored varieties.

3 Pinks and greens contrast in this delicate yet colorful design.

UNDERSTANDING
TEXTURE

While it can be a subtle design feature, texture offers a vital sensory element in a display. A plant's surface type determines how it interacts with light and shadow, which gives it a unique presence: for example, velvety leaves have a soft, matte appearance, while smooth, glossy foliage presents a crisp, bright, clean-cut image.

WHAT IS TEXTURE?

Texture describes a plant's foliage and the effect it creates when interacting with light and shadow. While it adds a seemingly tactile dimension, texture should primarily remain a visual design element: some plants, like the bunny ears cactus, may look soft, but you would not want to touch those fine spikes.

Feathery

Velvety, matte

Plump, fleshy

Smooth, glossy

Spiky, rough

HARMONY OF TEXTURE

When similar-textured plants are grouped together, the quality of light and shadow across their foliage is consistent, creating a relationship between the plants despite any other visual differences, such as color or size. This relationship unifies the display, creating a balanced whole and imparting a sense of simplicity.

Mistletoe cactus

"*Texture adds another dimension to your display through the visual qualities of the plant's leaves.*"

Baby's tears

Bunny ears cactus

Donkey's tail

CONTRAST OF TEXTURE

Strong textural contrasts create drama and interest.
The greater the contrast, the greater the emphasis
on each plant's individual presence: the clean,
crisp foliage of a glossy-leaved plant versus the
wild, informal appearance of feathered leaves,
for instance, or a succulent's plump, fleshy leaves
versus the spiky prickles of a cactus.

DESIGNING WITH HARMONY OF TEXTURE

When a group of plants interact with light in the same way—absorbing or reflecting it, offering similar textural patterns of light and dark—there is a unity achieved that brings the composition together as a whole. A thoughtful combination of similar textures offset by other contrasting elements creates interest, although too much repetition creates monotony.

1 Pairing the structurally different, but equally glossy, ZZ plant (left) and radiator plant (right) builds a strong relationship that is reinforced by similarly glossy containers.

2 The *Myrtillocactus* (left) and rat tail cactus (right) contrast in almost every regard, but their matching spiky textures offers a point of harmony.

3 A seemingly random sprawling group of air plants is given unity by the similarity of their textures.

4 Texture can harmonize a contrasting color palette, linking the two purple velvet plants with the *Echeveria* (left) and *Kalanchoe* (right).

"Light, feathery foliage carries less visual weight than denser, solid-leaved plants, so use more in a display if you want the different textures to appear balanced."

DESIGNING WITH
TEXTURE

Texture is the key to evoking mood in a display. Velvety, smooth, feathery, spiky: your choice of textures will set the tone for your arrangement and the mood of the space your plants will occupy. How you then reinforce that texture through harmony, or contrast it with a different texture, gives your design its focus and emphasis.

DESIGNING WITH CONTRAST OF TEXTURE

Bringing diverse textures together builds excitement and tension, as each texture brings a different mood to the display. The relationship between the different textures needs to be carefully balanced, however, in order not to simply suggest chaos. The light and shadow should work across the design in such a way that the eye is drawn to the contrasts but can also see the rhythm in them.

1 Fleshy, plump succulents contrast interestingly with the pretty fronds of moss; the voluptuousness of the succulents is accentuated by the delicacy of the carpet and reindeer mosses.

2 The dominant, rougher texture of the blue star fern's velvety leaves is sandwiched between the softer, more elegant Boston fern (left) and the fine foliage of the delta maidenhair fern (right).

UNDERSTANDING
CONTAINERS

An integral part of any houseplant arrangement is the choice of pots. While neutral containers can offer a unifying backdrop for your plants, a bold container choice that emphasizes one or more design elements can become a focal point in itself, emphasizing your plants' best features and tying them in with the surrounding environment.

SCALE

Containers that play with scale and proportion can change the relationship between identical plants, while matching containers of the same scale can unify a group of different plants.

SHAPE

A container's shape can harmonize or contrast with your plant's growing habit. It can echo and accentuate the natural shape of the plant, or contrast with it to create interest or drama.

"Like the accessories that tie together your favorite outfit, containers add those all-important finishing touches to your houseplant design."

COLOR

TEXTURE

Colors and patterns on a container can be used to highlight features in your plant. Stripes can echo stripes and color can pick up on color, highlighting what may have been a subtle accent on a plant.

The surface of your container can complement the texture of your plant's foliage, or directly contrast with it, in order to play on the differences and the sensory interest of the display.

"For an eye-catching display, hunt out interesting and unusual containers in vintage stores."

DESIGNING WITH
CONTAINERS

Be adventurous with your container choice. Almost anything can be used as a container or cachepot: as well as regular pots and terrariums, try repurposing old household items for a conversation-starting display.

1 This rustic white tray harmonizes with the dusty appearance of the air plants it displays.

2 A glass terrarium can display an entire miniature garden, allowing it to be admired from every angle.

3 These glass baubles act as tiny hanging terrariums for the ferns and trailing plants within.

4 Try planting spring bulbs in glass jars to show off their root systems as they grow.

5 Add drainage holes to the base of a clean food can to create a statement cacti container.

6 A vintage jug makes a curious decorative cachepot for an orchid.

7 Wall-mounted containers turn these two staghorn ferns into living pieces of art.

8 These classic, modern containers directly contrast with the appearance of the echeverias.

1

Use your imagination
With a little creative thinking, almost anything can be used for a display. This mismatched collection of glasses harmonizes with the succulents' foliage colors, and even shows off their soil and roots.

DESIGNING FOR BRIGHT LIGHT

If you're lucky enough to have lots of bright light in your home (see pp.180–81), take advantage of the possibilities by designing stunning displays of sun-loving plants. Fill up an empty window from top to bottom with lush greenery, or create a hanging garden beneath a skylight. Just remember to make sure your chosen plants can cope with the level of sunlight they are exposed to (see Plant Profiles, pp.100–75).

1 Combine a mixture of sun-loving plants of different sizes and shapes to create a windowsill display that makes the most of the bright light levels.

2 Propagated cuttings (see pp.96–99) make a pretty and practical display in a bright area out of direct sun.

3 Hang vanda orchids (see p.115) in front of a window to show off their roots, which can be displayed without potting soil.

4 In the wild, many orchids trail from high tree branches. Echo that by hanging them beneath a skylight, out of direct sun.

5 This colorful, multilevel orchid display fills a small window with blooms.

6 A hanging herb planter makes practical use of a kitchen window.

DESIGNING FOR
LOW LIGHT

Don't despair if your home does not receive a lot of bright daylight. Many plants prefer bright indirect light, and some can even thrive in areas of medium light (see pp.180–81), since many of them would naturally grow in the low light beneath a forest canopy. Use this as inspiration when designing for low light, adding touches of lush greenery to evoke a woodland landscape in your living space.

1 Large, glossy-leaved foliage and climbing plants trained up walls bring a touch of the jungle to an urban home.

2 Orchids that would naturally grow under dense forest canopies, such as this moth orchid, are well-suited to low light.

3 This small display of woodland plants will thrive in bright indirect light/medium light (L–R: blue star fern, baby's tears, Cretan brake fern).

4 Keep a bowl of wet pebbles near a collection of lush feathery forest ferns to keep them looking hydrated and fresh (L–R: crocodile fern, Boston fern).

5 Add flashes of color to a low-light display by using flowering plants and variegated leaves (such as those of a polka dot begonia, center).

DESIGNING FOR
HUMIDITY

Most moisture-loving plants need regular watering and care, but what if you could display them in a ready-made humid space in which they could thrive? Use humidity to your advantage and be adventurous in your designs: dare to turn a kitchen into a jungle, or take over the bathroom with ambitious living walls and displays, where the steam will naturally mist humidity-lovers like ferns, bromeliads, and air plants.

1 Contrast the bright foliage of a bathroom bromeliad display with the addition of a humidity-loving Amazonian elephant's ear.

2 Assemble a kokedama string garden (see pp.76–79) in humid areas of your home (L–R: Boston fern, spider plant, Cretan brake fern).

3 A trailing rosary vine adds a touch of atmosphere to a bathroom counter.

4 Use a humid spot to keep feathery foliage lush and fresh (L–R: baby's tears, Delta maidenhair fern, and string of pearls).

5 Since air plants draw moisture from the air, display them in a humid room in a wire frame or on a stand (see pp.56–59).

6 Carnivorous plants love moist, too-wet environments, so will thrive in a humid space.

DESIGNING FOR
SPACE

Any living space, large or small, offers plenty of opportunities to get creative with houseplant design. If you have no free surfaces, create a colony of hanging plants above your head. If you have bare walls, swap artwork for architectural displays of plant-filled shelves. With a little imagination, you will find more and more ways to turn any space into an indoor oasis.

1 If you want to hang nontrailing plants from the ceiling, use decorative containers that will look attractive from below. Hang climbing plants from rafters, if your home has them, to allow the foliage to grow up and along the beams.

2 Climbing plants aren't just for the garden; you can also train them to indoor walls to fill an empty space.

3 Fill a tall set of shelves with a curated selection of plants to create your own "green library."

4 Assemble a lush collection of hanging plants to create a "living curtain" of foliage.

5 Create a miniature garden in a tiny space using a terrarium (see pp.64–69 and pp.84–87). Display it at eye level, where the details can be closely admired.

6 Almost any space is up for grabs when designing plant displays. A staircase, for example, shows off your plants at eye level and from above as you walk down.

1

4

2

3

5

6

DESIGNING FOR
WELL-BEING

There is far more to houseplant design than visual beauty. Plants aren't just decorative objects: they are capable of lowering our stress levels, filling our homes with fragrance, and even ridding the air we breathe of harmful pollutants (see pp.46–47). Follow the advice on these pages to make the most of these benefits.

HOW HOUSEPLANTS HELP

Multiple studies have shown that there are tangible psychological benefits to keeping plants in indoor spaces such as homes and offices. After spending time living and working alongside plants, those taking part in the studies found that, on average:

- Their mood levels improved
- They felt less stressed
- They felt more productive
- Their attention span improved (in some studies)

DESIGNING FOR
MINDFULNESS

Modern life doesn't always offer enough opportunities to enjoy the great outdoors, especially for those of us living in built-up urban environments with little daily access to parks or forests. Studies have shown that living and working in a plant-filled environment can noticeably boost mental well-being (see below left). By adding touches of greenery throughout your home, especially in the places where you spend the most time, you will create a more calming atmosphere in which you can go about your daily life. In particular, keep plants near any windows that look out onto built-up areas to bring nature into your view.

1 A plant-filled home can provide a psychological boost when access to nature is otherwise limited. For the full effect, create an indoor jungle packed to the rafters with foliage to stimulate your mind and improve your mood.

DESIGNING FOR
THE SENSES

Fragrant houseplants add an extra sensory dimension to any plant design. We often bring bulbs and other scented plants into our homes during the darkest months of the year to remind ourselves of the sights and smells of spring. Position them in a front hallway for a bright, fragrant welcome, or near a door so that you will catch a hint of fragrance every time you pass.

1 Nelly Isler (left) and *Brassia* orchid blooms both provide a burst of scent.
2 *Stephanotis* is a classic plant choice when designing for scent.
3 Thyme bushes release a wonderful fragrance when brushed against in passing.
4 Combine scented and unscented plants to create a larger display without an overwhelming amount of fragrance (L–R: peace lily, scented hoya, scented cyclamen).
5 "Force" grape hyacinth bulbs for scent and color during winter (see pp.198–99).

DESIGNING FOR
AIR PURIFICATION

In addition to boosting our mood, houseplants can even improve our physical health and well-being by filtering harmful pollutants, including formaldehyde and benzene, from the air inside our homes and offices.

These chemicals, which are found in many everyday products—including cosmetics, soft furnishings, and detergents—are released into the atmosphere over time and may build up inside poorly ventilated buildings. This polluted air can, in high-enough quantities, lead to headaches; fatigue; and eye, nose, and throat irritation.

Luckily, houseplants can help. Studies have shown that plants are able to filter these pollutants from indoor air by drawing in the chemicals as they respire, leaving the air cleaner and healthier for us to breathe. What better excuse, then, than to fill your home with dozens of air-purifying plants?

Madagascar dragon tree

Peace lily

Chinese evergreen

Spider plant

THE BEST PLANTS FOR AIR PURIFICATION

While most plants are able to purify the air to some extent, some varieties are especially effective at removing certain chemicals from the air. These include:

For formaldehyde:

- Peace lily
- Chinese evergreen
- Areca palm

For both formaldehyde and benzene:

- Spider plant
- Madagascar dragon tree
- Snake plant
- India rubber plant
- Boston fern
- Golden pothos
- Dracaena lemon lime
- ZZ plant

For benzene:

- Jade tree
- Areca palm
- Cast iron plant
- Dumb cane
- Kentia palm

India rubber plant

Snake plants

Jade tree

Bring the outside in
Who needs a garden when you can create your own indoor oasis of lush greenery? This forest of foliage fills every available space with mood-boosting, air-purifying houseplants.

HOUSEPLANT PROJECTS

DESERTSCAPE

Grouping your cacti and succulent collection together in a single container is a great way to show off their different characteristics. The container does not have to be deep, as cacti have shallow root systems, but make sure it has adequate drainage; adding a layer of gravel beneath the potting soil will help prevent waterlogging if your container has no drainage holes.

WHAT YOU WILL NEED

PLANTS
- Selection of cacti, succulents, and plants with similar care needs, such as bunny ears cacti, golden ball cacti, and African spears

OTHER MATERIALS
- Shallow decorative container, preferably with drainage holes
- Fine-grade gravel
- Activated charcoal
- Cactus potting soil
- Pebbles and small stones, to decorate

TOOLS
- Small tray, for watering
- Spoon or small trowel
- Dibble
- Protective cactus gloves
- Small paintbrush, for dusting

1 Water the cacti and other plants thoroughly by placing them on a small tray filled with water. This will encourage the roots to make good contact with the new potting soil.

2 Pour a layer of gravel, approximately 1in (2.5cm) deep, into the base of the container. Mix in a few spoonfuls of activated charcoal to prevent the growth of fungi. Top with an even layer of cactus potting soil, 2–4in (5–7.5cm) deep.

3 While still in their pots, arrange the plants on top of the potting soil until you are happy with their placement. Allow plenty of room for growth. Once you like the arrangement, remove the plants, remembering where you intend to plant them.

4 Select your first plant. Using the dibble, make a hole large enough to accommodate the plant's root ball. Wearing gloves, remove the plant from its pot and gently tease the roots to release excess soil. Repeat for the remaining plants.

5 Using a spoon, carefully fill in any gaps between the plants with potting soil. Firm the soil down using the back of the spoon or the dibble.

6 Decorate the surface of the potting soil with pebbles and small stones.

HOW TO MAINTAIN

TEMPERATURE 50–86°F (10–30°C)
LIGHT High/Bright indirect in summer
HUMIDITY Low
CARE Easy

WATERING Water your cacti when the potting soil is completely dry. Depending on the conditions of your living space, this will usually take 3–4 weeks. Water thoroughly, but take care not to overwater, especially if your container does not have drainage holes, as this could cause root rot. Do not water at all between October and March.

MAINTENANCE AND CARE Gently brush off any potting soil caught in the spines of the plants with a soft paintbrush. Place on a sunny windowsill from fall to spring; move the display farther away from the window in summer, when the heat can become too intense. Watch out for drafts in winter, and relocate if necessary.

AIR PLANT STAND

Rootless air plants do not need soil to survive, and in the wild they are found clinging to rocky surfaces and hanging from the branches of trees. Echo their natural habitat by growing them on a wooden stand, which can comfortably display a small collection of air plants without using any glue or wire to hold them in place.

WHAT YOU WILL NEED

PLANTS
- Decorative mosses and lichen
- Selection of air plants in a variety of shapes, colors, and sizes (see pp.174–75)

OTHER MATERIALS
- Untreated, rugged piece of wood with plenty of crevices and hollows, such as driftwood, grapewood, cork bark, or tree fern
- Small branch
- Florist's wire

TOOLS
- Large bowl, for soaking
- Wire cutters
- Hot glue gun (optional)

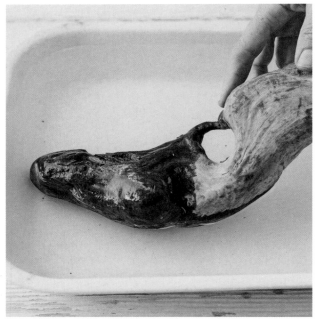

1 If using ocean driftwood, make sure it has been presoaked to remove all salt residue. To desalinate your own driftwood, soak it in freshwater for several weeks, replenishing the water a few times during this period.

2 Thread small pieces of moss onto the small branch and place it on top of the larger piece of wood. This will double up as both a decorative feature and an additional platform upon which to arrange your smaller air plants.

3 Fasten the branch to the wood with wire, wrapping it around at least a couple of times to ensure it is secure.

4 Attach bunches of moss and lichen to the larger piece of wood, using the wire or hot glue gun to secure them in place. If using glue, allow it to cool and solidify completely before adding your air plants to the display.

5 Gently arrange your air plants in the wood's natural crevices. Lighter, more delicate air plants can be placed along the attached branch. Do not glue the air plants in place (see right).

HOW TO MAINTAIN

TEMPERATURE 60-75°F (15-24°C)
LIGHT Bright indirect
HUMIDITY High
CARE Easy

WATERING Water your air plants with unsoftened water once a week (see p.185). Make sure the water is at lukewarm or at room temperature; cold water will shock the plants. Place them on a soft dishcloth and let them dry out completely before returning them to the stand. You can mist them 2-3 times a week.

MAINTENANCE AND CARE Place the stand in bright indirect light. Make sure young plants have room to grow; if they become too large for their current spot, move them to a roomier, more stable part of the stand.

Never use glue or wire to attach air plants to a display. Not only would this make it very difficult to soak the plants, but the chemicals in the glue may seriously harm the plants.

MACRAMÉ HANGER

Macramé, the art of decoratively knotting cords and rope, can be used
to create a simple hanger on which to display your favorite houseplants.
Use wooden beads and cotton cord to create the simple, modern look shown
here, or try different materials, such as metallic beads or unbleached rope,
to design a unique macramé hanger of your own.

WHAT YOU WILL NEED

PLANT
- Suitable plant in a 6in (15cm) pot, such
  as a delta maidenhair fern

OTHER MATERIALS
- 32ft (10m) strong, nonstretch cord
  or string, such as cotton cord
- Wooden ring
- S-hook
- 8 wooden beads (4 small and 4 large)
- Decorative cachepot suitable for
  a 6in (15cm) plant

TOOLS
- Ruler or tape measure
- Scissors

1 Cut 4 lengths of cotton cord measuring 7¼ft (220cm), and 2 lengths measuring 20in (50cm). Thread the 4 long cords through the wooden ring, folding them in half over the edge. Hold the cords together in one hand just below the ring, leaving the lengths trailing below.

2 Take one of the shorter cords and make a loop at one end. Pinch the loop in place on top of the trailing cords in your right hand, leaving both the long and short tails of the loop above the wooden ring.

3 Tightly wrap the long tail around the loop and trailing cords 5 times, moving farther away from the wooden ring. After 5 turns, thread the remainder of the long tail through the loop hole.

4 Pull the short tail so that the loop slides inside the 5 turns. Cut off both ends close to the binding and tuck inside to complete the knot. This technique is known as a "wrapping knot."

5 Using the S-hook, hang the ring up and check that you have 8 equal lengths of cord hanging down. Separate the cords into 4 pairs. Thread 1 small and 1 large wooden bead onto each pair of cords, approximately 12in (30cm) down from the ring.

6 Take 1 cord from 2 adjacent pairs and tie them together in a knot about 3in (8cm) down from the beads. Repeat this 3 times until all the cords are tied together. Repeat this process about 2in (6cm) below these knots (again taking 2 cords from adjacent pairs) to make another set of knots. The cords should now resemble a net.

7 Gather all the cords about 2in (6cm) below these knots. Using the second short length of cord, tie them together in another wrapping knot (see steps 2–4). Ensure this knot is as tight as possible, then trim any excess cord to the desired length.

8 Finally, fit your decorative cachepot securely into the hanger, then gently place your choice of plant inside the pot.

HOW TO MAINTAIN

WATERING When the plant needs watering, carefully remove it (and the pot) from the macramé hanger to prevent the cord from staining and rotting.

MAINTENANCE AND CARE Before displaying your plant, test its weight in the macramé hanger by gently lifting it up by the S-hook. The wrapping knots should hold firm; if the pot doesn't feel secure within the hanger, remove it and retie the knots until you are confident that they will hold.

As the plant grows, it will cascade beautifully over the sides of the hanger. If it becomes too large and needs repotting, replace it with another 6in (15cm) plant rather than squeezing it back into the hanger in its larger pot.

OPEN-BOTTLE TERRARIUM

A terrarium is a semi-enclosed glass container that creates a warm, humid microclimate for the plants that grow within. For this open-bottle terrarium, choose a selection of foliage plants that showcase a variety of leaf shapes and colors. Pick one large "feature" plant that will stand out from the rest, taking care not to overcrowd the bottle so that they all have room to grow.

WHAT YOU WILL NEED

PLANTS
- Selection of humidity-loving foliage plants (including 1 larger focal plant), such as small ferns, peperomias, and fittonias
- Decorative mosses (optional)

OTHER MATERIALS
- Wide, open-topped, heavy glass bottle or jar
- Fine-grade gravel
- Activated charcoal
- Multipurpose potting soil
- Decorative pebbles (optional)

EQUIPMENT
- Dibble
- Small watering can with a rose attachment

1 Pour a layer of gravel, approximately 1in (2.5cm) deep, into the base of the bottle for drainage. Mix in a few spoonfuls of activated charcoal to prevent the growth of fungi.

2 Add an even layer of potting soil, 2–4in (5–7.5cm) deep, over the gravel-charcoal mixture. Make a hole in the soil the same size as the focal plant's root ball.

3 Remove the focal plant from its pot and loosen the roots to encourage healthy growth. Gently place the plant in the hole.

4 Firm the potting soil around the base of the plant using the dibble. Repeat steps 3–4 with your remaining plants.

5 If you wish, cover the surface of the potting soil with decorative mosses or pebbles. Carefully wipe the inside of the bottle clean.

HOW TO MAINTAIN

WATERING Use a small watering can fitted with a rose attachment to water the plants. The grouped plants and semi-enclosed space create a humid environment that traps moisture, so take care not to overwater. Only water the plants when the potting soil dries out.

MAINTENANCE AND CARE Place the terrarium in a bright spot, but out of direct sunlight, which may scorch the leaves through the glass.

WILLOW CLIMBING FRAME

This simple support for climbing plants is quick and easy to assemble, and makes an attractive feature even before it is hidden by leafy plant growth. Once you've mastered this basic frame, you can apply the technique to more ambitious climbing projects by training the plant's stems onto a trellis room divider or staircase, or fanning them out across a wall.

WHAT YOU WILL NEED

PLANT
- Climbing plant, such as a philodendron, hoya, jasmine, or stephanotis

OTHER MATERIALS
- Heavy-based pot with drainage holes
- Multipurpose potting soil
- 7 pliable willow poles, each at least 3ft (1m) in length
- Garden twine

TOOLS
- Garden scissors

1 Fill your pot with potting soil. Insert 6 evenly spaced willow poles around the edge of the pot.

2 Gather the poles together at a comfortable height directly above the centre of the pot, and tie together securely with a length of twine. Trim away any excess length from the tops of the poles using garden scissors.

3 Weave the final length of willow through the poles, roughly one-third of the way up the stand. Secure in place with twine to prevent it from slipping, then remove the entire frame from the pot and place it to one side.

4 Make a hole in the potting soil the size of the root ball and lower the plant in, ensuring it sits at the same level that it rested at in its original pot. Fill in any gaps with new potting soil, firming it down gently.

6 One by one, wrap and weave the long stems of the plant around the poles. Thicker or heavier stems may need to be tied in with the twine; take care not to tie it too tightly.

HOW TO MAINTAIN

WATERING Keep the compost moist from spring to fall; reduce in winter, watering when the top of the compost feels dry. Mist every few days in summer, or when necessary.

MAINTENANCE AND CARE As the plant grows, continue to weave the stems around the willow poles, tying them in with twine where necessary. If the plant climbs higher than the frame, most can be pruned to keep the size in check and the plant compact.

Alternatively, position the overgrown plant next to a trellis and weave the longer stems onto the frame, training it over time and securing with garden twine.

5 Spread the untangled stems of the climber out in a fan around the base of the pot. Insert the willow frame back into the potting soil, over the stems.

SUCCULENT WREATH

Plant an assortment of small succulent plants into a ring of carpet moss to create a beautiful and unique decorative wreath that will require minimal care when kept in the right conditions. Pair a variety of succulents with several different types of fluffy moss to add interest and character to your display.

WHAT YOU WILL NEED

PLANTS
- Carpet moss
- Selection of approximately 12 mini succulent plants, each with a 2in (5cm) pot size, such as echeverias, sempervivums, aeoniums, and crassulas
- Reindeer moss

OTHER MATERIALS
- Florist's wire wreath frame, 12in (30cm) in diameter
- Potting soil
- Florist's mossing pins
- Florist's wire

TOOLS
- Tray, for soaking
- Wire cutters
- Mister spray (optional)

1 Soak the carpet moss in a tray of water to make it easier to work with.

2 Line the wire wreath frame with the carpet moss. Make sure that the bottom and sides of the frame are covered, and that you have enough moss to fold over the root balls of the plants.

3 Remove the plants from their pots and loosen their roots. Fold back the moss and bed the plants into the frame, allowing plenty of room for the plants to grow. Fill in the empty spaces between the plants with potting soil.

4 Fold the carpet moss back into place, over and around the bases of the plants and potting soil.

5 Use the florist's pins to secure the moss firmly in place around the base of the plants. Push the pins all the way down into the soil, so the moss holds tightly in place.

6 For extra security, wrap florist's wire around your wreath to stop the moss unraveling as it beds down.

7 Finally, cover any exposed areas of soil or wire with pieces of reindeer moss, firmly pinning them in place.

HOW TO MAINTAIN

WATERING Depending on the heat and the humidity of the room, water the display approximately once a week by submerging the mossy base in a sink full of water. Let the wreath fully dry out before soaking it again. If the air is very dry, mist the plants occasionally.

MAINTENANCE AND CARE Place your wreath out of direct sunlight and heat. Keep it laid flat for 1–2 months as the roots settle in. After this period, it will be safe to hang your wreath upright if you wish.

KOKEDAMA FERN

A type of bonsai, "kokedama" is the practice of suspending the roots of a plant in a mud ball coated with soft green moss. It is a great way to make a beautiful, hanging, sculptural object with a live plant. Arranging many kokedama plants together forms what is known as a "string garden."

WHAT YOU WILL NEED

PLANTS
- Mature fern, such as a Cretan brake, foxtail, or staghorn fern
- Sheet of carpet moss

OTHER MATERIALS
- Potting soil
- Akadama (claylike mineral used in bonsai)
- Garden twine

TOOLS
- Bucket
- Scissors
- Mister spray

1 Create a 2:1 mixture of potting soil and akadama in a bucket, adding a little water until it reaches a sticky, wet consistency. The akadama turns the soil into a "mud-cake" that will mold around the plant's roots.

2 Take the fern from its pot and gently shake loose some of the original potting soil from its roots.

3 Encase the fern roots in a layer of the damp potting soil–akadama mixture, approximately 1in (2.5cm) thick. Aim to create a ball of about the same volume as the original pot.

4 Envelop the root ball in a sheet of carpet moss, gathering the moss around the stem.

5 Trim the excess moss with a pair of scissors, leaving some behind at the neck of the root ball.

6 Wrap twine around the neck of the moss ball to secure the moss in place. Knot the twine firmly. To hang the fern up, attach a second length of twine around the neck of the kokedama to form a loop.

HOW TO MAINTAIN

TEMPERATURE 55–75°F (13–75°C)
LIGHT Bright indirect/Medium
HUMIDITY Moderate
CARE Average

WATERING Check if your plant needs to be watered by testing the weight of the moss ball. When it feels light, submerge the kokedama ball in water, keeping the foliage dry. Allow it to soak for 10–25 minutes, or until it is fully saturated. Remove the kokedama from the bucket, and gently squeeze the ball to drain any excess water.

MAINTENANCE AND CARE Place your kokedama in a humid spot with bright indirect light. Mist regularly using a spray bottle.

MOSS PICTURE FRAME

Living walls and vertical gardens have become increasingly popular in urban homes around the world. You can easily make one at home using a selection of mosses and mosslike plants, or alternatively with air plants. Creating a moss arrangement is all about combining various textures and colors to mimic a landscape.

WHAT YOU WILL NEED

PLANTS
- Variety of different mosses, such as sphagnum moss to use as a foundation, bun moss to create hills and dips, and more decorative types like reindeer moss or trailing Spanish moss
- Mosslike plants, such as baby's tears (see p.140)

OTHER MATERIALS
- Repurposed shallow wooden container, such as a wine crate or old serving tray, with a depth of approximately 4in (10cm)
- Plastic trash can liner
- Florist's pins
- Decorative branches, such as twigs with lichens growing on them and small pieces of driftwood
- Florist's wire

TOOLS
- Stapler or staple gun
- Wire cutters
- Watering can with a rose attachment or mister spray

1 Line the back of the wooden container with a plastic trash can liner, stapling it into place. This will help retain moisture within the frame.

2 Working on a flat surface, staple or pin a thin layer of sphagnum moss to the back of the container to completely cover the plastic.

3 Arrange pieces of bun moss in the container to add texture and interest. Pin to the sphagnum moss using florist's pins. Begin adding pieces of decorative mosses to the display as desired.

4 Remove your mosslike plants from their pots and loosen the roots. Bed the plants down between mounds of bun moss.

5 For extra interest, attach pieces of decorative moss to twigs and small branches using wire, then place them into the display by wedging them securely into the lower corners of the frame.

6 Add a few final pieces of decorative moss to the display as desired, combining different colors and textures to mimic a landscape. Secure them discreetly to the twigs using wire.

HOW TO MAINTAIN

WATERING Lightly water or mist the moss frame every few days. If dry air or central heating dries the plant out, you can also completely soak the moss to revive it.

MAINTENANCE AND CARE Keep the frame laid flat for 1-2 months to allow the moss and rooted plants to settle into place. After that time, you can prop up the display or hang it upright if you wish.

As with all photosynthetic organisms, your moss wall will prefer a room with high humidity and indirect light.

DRY TERRARIUM

Unlike the humidity-loving plants displayed in the open-bottle terrarium (see pp.64–67), the plants in this display prefer drier, desertlike conditions. Choose a selection of succulents and cacti that vary in height and shape to create a more interesting display. This open terrarium does not self-irrigate, and so must be watered occasionally.

WHAT YOU WILL NEED

PLANTS
- Selection of plants (including 1 larger focal plant), such as echeveria, crassula, and haworthia

OTHER MATERIALS
- Glass terrarium with an opening of at least 7in (18cm)
- Gravel or small pebbles
- Activated charcoal
- Cactus potting soil
- Decorative pebbles

TOOLS
- Dibble
- Small trowel or spoon
- Watering can

1 Pour a shallow layer of gravel, with a depth of approximately 1in (2.5cm), over the base of the terrarium. Mix a small handful of activated charcoal into the gravel.

2 Add a layer of cactus potting soil, approximately 2–4in (5–7.5cm) deep, on top of the gravel–charcoal mixture.

3 Select your focal plant and remove it from its pot. Gently loosen the roots to encourage growth.

4 Make a hole in the potting soil the same size as the root ball and gently place the plant in it. Use the dibble to firm the potting soil around the base of the plant.

5 Repeat this process with 2–3 smaller plants. Leave space between the plants to allow for both growth and good air flow. This will prevent a build-up of humidity between the plants, which could lead to rot.

6 Once the plants are firmly in place, carefully place decorative pebbles on top of the soil using a spoon.

HOW TO MAINTAIN

WATERING Only water your display occasionally, when the potting soil completely dries out. The semi-enclosed space of the terrarium will retain moisture and create humidity, so take care not to overwater, as this may cause rot.

MAINTENANCE AND CARE Place your terrarium in indirect light; bright light could magnify within the glass container and cause the plants to overheat and dry out.

WOOD-MOUNTED ORCHID

Mounting an orchid on decorative wood makes a beautiful display and can be beneficial to your orchid's health. It mimics how the orchid would grow naturally and allows for good drainage and ventilation to the roots, which will help your plant thrive and prevent disease.

WHAT YOU WILL NEED

PLANTS
- Small orchid, such as a moth orchid or nobile dendrobium
- Sphagnum and decorative mosses

OTHER MATERIALS
- Decorative piece of wood, such as driftwood, tree bark, cork bark, or birch pole
- Florist's wire

TOOLS
- Wire cutters

1 Remove the orchid from its pot and carefully tease the potting medium from its roots.

2 Pack sphagnum moss evenly in and around the roots of the orchid, leaving some outer roots partially exposed. Gently secure in place with a little wire.

3 Position the orchid on the piece of wood with the plant's crown angled downward. Wrap the wire around the base and roots of the orchid to secure it to the wood.

4 Take care not to wrap the wire around the orchid too tightly, as this could damage it. When the plant feels comfortably secure, twist the two ends of wire together and cut away the excess with wire cutters.

5 Decorate the rest of the piece of wood with additional handfuls of moss, using wire to secure them in place.

HOW TO MAINTAIN

TEMPERATURE 61-80°F (16-27°C)
LIGHT Bright indirect/Medium
HUMIDITY Moderate to high
CARE Easy

WATERING Orchids attached to mounts tend to dry out fairly quickly, so water at least three times a week. To water the plant, submerge the entire mount in a large, deep bowl for 20 minutes until completely saturated.

MAINTENANCE AND CARE Place in a humid area and mist daily. Leave the wire intact while the orchid's roots find secure purchase on the wood. The root moss will eventually fall away as the plant grows new roots and explores the wood's surface. Over time, the plant will develop the elegant, flattened shape characteristic of orchids found in the wild.

LIVING SPACE DIVIDER

A movable trailing plant space divider can be used to create a beautiful temporary wall or living screen between different parts of your indoor space. Choose bushier plants to fill out the divider more completely, or show off a selection of decorative containers using macramé hangers (see pp.60–63).

WHAT YOU WILL NEED

PLANTS
- Selection of trailing plants that prefer bright, indirect light, such as string of pearls, rosary vine, and Christmas cacti
- Selection of tall, midsized foliage plants with similar requirements, such as fiddle-leaf figs, spider plants, and most ferns

OTHER MATERIALS
- Free-standing clothes rack, ideally with a lower shelf
- String
- S-hooks
- Decorative cachepots of appropriate sizes
- Macramé hangers
- Large pot or bucket

TOOLS
- Scissors
- Watering can

1 Select your first trailing plant. If its plastic pot is hidden by foliage, make 3 evenly spaced holes through the rim of the pot with a pair of scissors. Thread a length of string through each hole, securing each in place with a firm knot.

2 Gather the three strings together directly above the center of the plant, at the length from which you want the plant to hang from the rack. Tie a secure knot, leaving a short length of string above.

3 Form a small loop with the excess string, and tie it to the existing knot as tightly and neatly as possible. Trim any remaining string with scissors.

4 Slip the bottom curve of an S-hook through the loop and slowly lift the plant, checking that all the knots are secure. Clip the top curve of the S-hook over the bar of the clothes rack. Repeat for all the plants you wish to hang.

5 If you wish to hide a plastic pot from view, place the plant in a decorative cachepot and nestle it securely into a macramé hanger. Tie the hanger securely onto the rack, or use an S-hook to hold it in place.

6 Once the rack is full, fill the gaps beneath by arranging a second selection of plants on the shelf beneath. Try out different combinations of plants and decorative pots until you are happy with the final appearance of your living frame.

HOW TO MAINTAIN

WATERING Water and mist all plants as required. Remove plants from macramé hangers when watering them to prevent saturating the decorative cord or rope (which could lead to rot over time).

MAINTENANCE AND CARE Wherever you position your room divider, ensure that the space is draft free. Prune plants as needed; swap them out if they grow too large for the display.

PROPAGATION SHELF

Rooting plants in water in pretty glass vessels makes a great display on a shelf or side table. You can make a temporary display while propagating cuttings to plant up later (see p.204), or leave them as they are to create a permanent "water garden." This method is very simple but not suited to all plants, so choose your cuttings carefully.

WHAT YOU WILL NEED

PLANTS
- Cuttings from mature, healthy plants, such as tradescantia, philodendron, crassula, pilea, epiphyllum, begonia, and chlorophytum

OTHER MATERIALS
- Glass bottles or vases of different heights and shapes; flasklike vessels with narrow necks and large bodies work best
- Unsoftened water, such as mineral water or rainwater

TOOLS
- Small pair of pruning shears or scissors

1 Select your first cutting. Measure it against the bottle in which you wish to display it, then remove any leaves from the portion of the stem that will be submerged in water.

2 If taking a cutting of a plant's offset, such as a "baby spider" from a spider plant (see p.207), make the cut at the base of the offset's individual stem. This is where the rooting hormone is most concentrated in the plant.

3 Half-fill your bottle with unsoftened water (do not use tap water). Make sure to use a glass bottle with plenty of room, so that the roots receive plenty of light and have space to grow.

4 Place the cutting in the vase and leave it undisturbed on your chosen propagation shelf. Repeat this process with your remaining cuttings, each matched to a proportionally sized glass bottle or vase, until your display is complete.

HOW TO MAINTAIN

WATERING Top up the bottles and vases with more water as and when needed.

MAINTENANCE AND CARE After just a few weeks, your cuttings will begin to sprout roots. At this stage, if you want to plant your propagated cuttings, follow the instructions on p.204.

You can also keep the cuttings permanently in water. If you choose to do so, remember to change the water or trim back the roots after a year or so.

PLANT PROFILES

BROMELIADS

These colorful plants bloom for many months and add a hint of the tropics to any bright room. They grow on trees in their native habitat, deriving moisture and nutrients from the air rather than soil, but they do not require exceptionally high humidity levels and are quite easy to care for. After blooming, the plants die back, but most bromeliads produce "baby" offsets (see pp.206–07) next to the base of the old leaves, which then grow into new plants. The original bromeliad plant rarely reblooms indoors.

AMAZONIAN ZEBRA PLANT
Aechmea chantinii

TEMPERATURE 59–80°F (15–27°C)
LIGHT Bright indirect/Medium
HUMIDITY Moderate
CARE Easy
HEIGHT & SPREAD 2 x 2ft (60 x 60cm)

This dramatic plant's dark green and silver striped leaves and tall flower spikes appear from late spring to fall. The blooms are composed of red, orange, and yellow bracts (petal-like modified leaves) and small red flowers.

WATERING Fill the cuplike well in the center of the leaf rosette with unsoftened water; replenish every 4–8 weeks. Keep the potting soil moist, but allow it to dry out between waterings in winter. Mist the plant when the humidity is low.

FEEDING From spring to fall, apply a half-strength balanced liquid fertilizer once a month.

PLANTING AND CARE Grow in an equal mix of orchid potting medium, perlite, and coconut fiber (or a 50:50 mix of orchid and multipurpose potting soils) in a 5–6in (12.5–15cm) pot. Repot young plants in a container one size larger.

SILVER VASE PLANT
Aechmea fasciata AGM

TEMPERATURE 59–80°F (15–27°C)
LIGHT Bright indirect/Medium
HUMIDITY Moderate
CARE Easy
HEIGHT & SPREAD 2 x 2ft
(60 x 60cm)

The elegant arching silver and green leaves offer reason enough to grow this beautiful plant. In summer, a tall flower spike appears, topped with delicate pink bracts and small purple flowers that add to its star quality.

WATERING Fill the well in the center of the leaf rosette with unsoftened water; replenish every 4–8 weeks. Keep the potting soil moist; allow it to dry out between waterings in winter. Mist the plant when the humidity is low.

FEEDING From spring to fall, apply a half-strength balanced liquid fertilizer once a month.

PLANTING AND CARE Grow in a 5–6in (12.5–15cm) pot in an equal mix of orchid potting medium, perlite, and coconut fiber (or a 50:50 mix of orchid and multipurpose potting soils). Repot young plants in a container one size larger.

VARIEGATED PINEAPPLE
Ananas comosus var. variegatus

TEMPERATURE 60–85°F (16–29°C)
LIGHT Sun/High
HUMIDITY Moderate
CARE Easy
HEIGHT & SPREAD At least
2 x 3ft (60 x 90cm)

Show-stopping, spiny-edged, green and cream foliage and pretty yellow and purple flowers make up for the fact that this pineapple's red fruits are bitter and inedible. It will be a nice feature in any sunny room, but check that you have space for its wide, arching leaves.

WATERING Wait until the soil dries out before watering. The soil should be moist, but never soggy. When the humidity is low, set on a tray of wet pebbles.

FEEDING From spring to fall, apply a half-strength balanced liquid fertilizer once a month.

PLANTING AND CARE Plant in an equal mix of fine composted bark or orchid potting medium, perlite, and coconut fiber (or a 50:50 mix of orchid and multipurpose potting soils). A heavy 5–6in (12.5–15cm) pot will restrict the plant's size. Repot in early spring in a container one size larger.

EARTH STAR
Cryptanthus bivittatus AGM

TEMPERATURE 60–80°F (16–27°C)
LIGHT Bright indirect
HUMIDITY Moderate
CARE Easy
HEIGHT & SPREAD 6 x 6in (15 x 15cm)

This dainty bromeliad is grown for its wavy, tooth-edged leaves, which form a flat, star-shaped rosette. Ideal for decorating a sunny windowsill in a small room, the colorful foliage—which can be red, orange, purple, pink, or green—makes a sparkling feature.

WATERING In spring and summer, use unsoftened water to keep the potting soil moist, but not soggy. In winter, keep it barely moist. Mist the plant regularly with unsoftened water.

FEEDING From spring to fall, apply a half-strength balanced liquid fertilizer once a month.

PLANTING AND CARE Plant in a small 4in (10cm) pot in an equal mix of orchid potting medium, perlite, and coconut fiber (or a 50:50 mix of orchid and multipurpose potting soils). Set in bright indirect light, and repot every 2–3 years in the spring.

QUEEN'S TEARS
Billbergia nutans

TEMPERATURE 60–80°F (16–27°C)
LIGHT Bright indirect/Medium
HUMIDITY High
CARE Easy
HEIGHT & SPREAD 2 x 2ft (60 x 60cm)

Set this bromeliad on a stand or in a hanging basket so that the graceful flowers can flow down over the edges. The plant's pink bracts (petal-like modified leaves) and small pink and purple blooms appear from late spring to summer among a fountain of gray-green strappy leaves.

WATERING Use unsoftened water to keep the potting soil moist. In winter, allow the top of the potting soil to dry out between waterings. Mist daily in summer, then reduce to every few days in winter.

FEEDING In early spring, add a teaspoon of Epsom salts diluted in unsoftened water to encourage flowering. From spring to fall, apply a half-strength balanced liquid plant food once a month.

PLANTING AND CARE Plant in an equal mix of orchid potting medium, perlite, and coconut fiber (or a 50:50 mix of orchid and multipurpose potting soils) in a 5–6in (12.5–15cm) pot. Repot young plants in early spring in a container one size larger.

ZEBRA PLANT
Cryptanthus zonatus

TEMPERATURE 60–80°F (16–27°C)
LIGHT High/Bright indirect
HUMIDITY Moderate
CARE Easy
HEIGHT & SPREAD Up to 10 x16in (25 x 40cm)

Prized for its striped, spidery-looking burgundy and cream leaves, the zebra plant makes a dramatic focal point when set alongside other small leafy plants that like similar conditions. Small white flowers may appear in summer on mature plants.

WATERING From spring to early fall, keep the potting soil moist with unsoftened water. The potting soil should be barely moist in winter. Mist the plant with unsoftened water every few days.

FEEDING In spring and summer, apply a half-strength basic houseplant fertilizer once a week.

PLANTING AND CARE Plant in an equal mix of orchid potting medium, perlite, and coconut fiber (or a 50:50 mix of orchid and multipurpose potting soils) in a small 4–5in (10–12.5cm) pot. Set in morning sun or bright indirect light; the plant may lose its variegations in low-light conditions. Repot zebra plants every 2–3 years in spring.

SCARLET STAR
Guzmania lingulata

TEMPERATURE 65–80°F (18–27°C)
LIGHT Bright indirect
HUMIDITY High
CARE Easy
HEIGHT & SPREAD 18 x 18in
(45 x 45cm)

The eye-catching flower spike of this compact bromeliad shoots up from the glossy green leaves like a firework. Its small white or yellow blooms are protected by long-lasting bright orange or red bracts.

WATERING Allow the potting soil to dry out between waterings, and fill the leafy cup in the center of the plant with unsoftened water, replenishing it every 4–7 days. Mist the leaves, flowers, and aerial roots daily with unsoftened water.

FEEDING Apply a half-strength balanced fertilizer to the central cup once a month. Pour this out after 4–5 days and replace with unsoftened water. When not in flower, mist the leaves once a month with the same fertilizer, diluted to one-quarter strength.

PLANTING AND CARE Use an equal mix of orchid potting medium, perlite, and coconut fiber (or a 50:50 mix of orchid and multipurpose potting soils) in a 4–5in (10–12.5cm) pot. Repot young plants each spring in fresh potting soil.

BLUSHING BROMELIAD
Neoregelia carolinae f. *tricolor*

TEMPERATURE 65–80°F (18–27°C)
LIGHT Bright indirect
HUMIDITY Moderate to high
CARE Easy
HEIGHT & SPREAD 12 x 24in
(30 x 60cm)

Like a blushing bride, this plant's leafy rosette of green and yellow striped leaves is suffused with red at the center. In summer, violet flowers and bright red bracts appear.

WATERING Fill the central well formed by the leaves with unsoftened water; replenish every 4–6 weeks. Keep the potting soil moist, but not soggy, and mist the leaves every few days.

FEEDING Mist the leaves monthly with a half-strength balanced liquid fertilizer. Overfeeding reduces the leaf color.

PLANTING AND CARE Plant in a small 4–5in (10–12.5cm) pot using an equal mix of orchid potting medium, perlite, and coconut fiber (or a 50:50 mix of orchid and multipurpose potting soils). Repot every year in fresh potting soil.

FLAMING SWORD
Vriesea splendens AGM

TEMPERATURE 64–79°F (18–26°C)
LIGHT Bright indirect
HUMIDITY Moderate
CARE Easy
HEIGHT & SPREAD 24 x 18in (60 x 45cm)

This plant's dark green and reddish-brown striped leaves and long-lasting, swordlike flowers make a striking partnership. The scarlet bracts envelop small yellow flowers, and can appear at any time of year. This is a relatively easy bromeliad for beginners to try.

WATERING Top up the central well formed by the leaves with unsoftened water; replenish every 2–3 weeks. Water when the top of the potting soil feels dry; keep it barely moist in winter. Mist every few days with unsoftened water.

FEEDING Dilute a foliar fertilizer to one-quarter strength and use it to spray the leaves monthly from spring to fall.

PLANTING AND CARE Plant in a 5–6in (12.5–15cm) pot in an equal mix of fine composted bark or orchid potting medium, perlite, and coconut fiber (or a 50:50 mix of orchid and multipurpose potting soils). Repot young plants into containers one size larger in early spring.

BULBOUS PLANTS

From tropical woodland plants to classic spring garden favorites, these flowers inject splashes of seasonal color and scent into indoor displays. Although bulbs are often associated with spring, many bloom at other times of the year—even in winter—so with a little planning, you can enjoy flowers in your home in every season. Just remember to plant the bulbs a few months before you want them to bloom.

CLIVIA
Clivia miniata AGM

TEMPERATURE 50–73°F (10–23°C)
LIGHT Bright indirect
HUMIDITY Low to moderate
CARE Average
HEIGHT & SPREAD 18 x 12in (45 x 30cm)
 WARNING! Bulbs are toxic

Brighten up your home in spring with the clivia's sunny orange, yellow, or apricot flowers. The clusters of trumpet-shaped blooms last until summer, and these pretty woodland plants will thrive in a cool, bright room.

WATERING Allow the top of the potting soil to dry out between waterings from spring until fall. The plant needs a rest from late fall to midwinter, when the potting soil should be kept almost dry.

FEEDING Once bloomed (usually early summer), apply a half-strength balanced liquid fertilizer once a month to early fall.

PLANTING AND CARE In fall, plant in a 50:50 mix of aerated and multipurpose potting soils in a 8in (20cm) pot, with the neck of the bulbs above the surface. Plants need a cool rest at 50°F (10°C) from midfall to late winter; then move to a well-lit room at 60°F (16°C) to bloom. Repot every 3–4 years; if top heavy and falling over, use a tall, heavy pot.

LILY OF THE VALLEY
Convallaria majalis AGM

TEMPERATURE -4–75°F (-20–24°C)
LIGHT Bright indirect/Medium
HUMIDITY Low
CARE Average
HEIGHT & SPREAD Up to 10 x 8in
(25 x 20cm)
WARNING! All parts are toxic

This dainty bulb's white, bell-shaped flowers will fill your home with sweet perfume when they appear in spring. The blooms are set off by bright green, spear-shaped leaves.

WATERING Keep the potting soil moist from late winter to early summer; when dormant from late summer to early winter, allow the potting soil to dry out.

FEEDING Feed monthly a half-strength balanced liquid fertilizer from late winter to early summer.

PLANTING AND CARE Plant the bulbs, with the roots down, in a deep 6–8in (15–20cm) pot of aerated potting soil, so they are just covered. See p.199 to force them to flower indoors. When in bud, set in a cool room at 60–70°F (16–21°C) to bloom. After the leaves die down, plant in shade outside; they need a cold period to reflower.

SIAM TULIP
Curcuma alismatifolia

TEMPERATURE 65–75°F (18–24°C)
LIGHT Bright indirect
HUMIDITY Moderate to high
CARE Average
HEIGHT & SPREAD 2 x 2ft (60 x 60cm)

This beauty from Thailand brings a touch of the tropics to your home in summer, when its tulip-shaped pink and violet flowers appear on tall stems between dark green leaves. Consider the needs of the plant before placing it in an area of your home or office.

WATERING From late spring to late summer, keep the potting soil moist, and set on a tray of wet pebbles to maintain the humidity. From midfall to early spring, the plant becomes dormant (the leaves will die off), and the potting soil should be almost dry.

FEEDING Apply a balanced liquid fertilizer every 2 weeks from midspring to late summer.

PLANTING AND CARE In spring, add a layer of gravel to a medium-sized 6in (15cm) pot, and top with a layer of bulb potting soil. Plant the bulbs 3in (7.5cm) below the potting soil surface. Place in a bright area out of direct sun. Cut off old flower stems and dying leaves in fall. Repot annually in spring in fresh potting soil.

AMARYLLIS
Hippeastrum hybrids

TEMPERATURE 55–70°F (13–21°C)
LIGHT Bright indirect
HUMIDITY Low
CARE Easy
HEIGHT & SPREAD 2 x 1ft (60 x 30cm)
WARNING! Bulbs are toxic

Give this striking plant pride of place when its trumpet-shaped flowers appear from winter to spring. Choose from white, pink, red, and orange blooms, or varieties with bicolored or patterned petals.

WATERING Water sparingly from early winter until the new leaves develop, then keep the potting soil moist while in bloom. Do not water when the plant is resting from late summer to late fall.

FEEDING Feed monthly a half-strength fertilizer high in potassium and phosphorus and low in nitrogen—5-10-10 or 6-12-12.

PLANTING AND CARE In late fall or winter, plant in multipurpose potting soil in a pot slightly larger than the bulb, with one-third of the bulb above the surface. Set in a bright, warm spot. Leaves, then flowers, appear 6–8 weeks later. Move to a cooler area when buds appear to prolong the flowering period. In late summer, let the bulbs dry out, repot, and set in a frost-free shed or garage for 2 months, then bring back indoors and resume watering.

HYACINTH
Hyacinthus orientalis

TEMPERATURE 5–68°F (-15–20°C)
LIGHT Bright indirect
HUMIDITY Low
CARE Average
HEIGHT & SPREAD 10 x 8in
(25 x 20cm)
WARNING! All parts are toxic

The intense perfume and rich colors of this classic spring-flowering bulb make it a favorite for indoor displays. Plant prepared hyacinth bulbs in fall to enjoy the spikes of blue, purple, white, pink, or red blooms when they open a few months later.

WATERING After planting the bulbs, water the potting soil and leave to drain. Keep barely moist throughout winter, and then consistently moist when the shoots and flowers appear.

FEEDING Apply a liquid seaweed fertilizer every 2 weeks, when leaves are dying down, if you want to keep the bulbs.

PLANTING AND CARE Plant bulbs in pots of bulb soil (or a 2:1 mix of aerated potting soil and sharp hard sand) in early fall, with the pointed ends up and just showing above the surface. Leave outside on a balcony or in the garden until ready to flower in midspring. To force bulbs, see pp.198–99.

GRAPE HYACINTH
Muscari species

TEMPERATURE 5–68°F (-15–20°C)
LIGHT Bright indirect
HUMIDITY Low
CARE Average
HEIGHT & SPREAD 8 x 4in (20 x 10cm)

This easy-to-grow bulb is a top choice for spring color, with its dainty little cones of lightly fragrant blue, purple, or white flowers and grassy foliage. These bulbs can be forced for early-season displays indoors.

WATERING Water bulbs after planting, and keep the potting soil almost dry in winter. The potting soil should be moist when the shoots and flowers appear.

FEEDING Apply a balanced liquid fertilizer every 2 weeks after flowering, while the leaves are dying down.

PLANTING AND CARE Fill a pot at least 6in (15cm) wide and deep with multipurpose potting soil. Plant the bulbs, pointed ends up, close together but not touching, and leave the tips just exposed. Set outside on a balcony or in a sheltered area until ready to flower, or force the bulbs for earlier displays (see pp.198–99). After blooming, set outside in shade; they will then reflower the following year.

DAFFODIL
Narcissus species

TEMPERATURE 5–68°F (-15–20°C)
LIGHT Bright indirect
HUMIDITY Low
CARE Easy
HEIGHT & SPREAD 16 x 4in
(40 x 10cm)
WARNING! All parts are toxic

The most popular daffodil for indoor gardens is the tender, scented paperwhite, but other hardy *Narcissus*, such as the perfumed Tazetta varieties or popular 'Tête-à-tête', also flower well inside. Plant the bulbs in fall for spring flowers.

WATERING Water bulbs after planting, and keep the potting soil barely moist through winter. Water every few days when the shoots and flowers appear.

FEEDING Apply a balanced liquid fertilizer every 2 weeks after flowering, while the leaves are dying down.

PLANTING AND CARE Add a layer of gravel to the bottom of a wide pot, and top up with bulb soil (or a 2:1 mix of aerated potting soil and sharp hard sand). Plant bulbs with the pointed ends up and the tips just below the surface. Set in an unheated room on a sunny windowsill.

FALSE SHAMROCK
Oxalis triangularis

TEMPERATURE 60–70°F (15–21°C)
LIGHT Medium
HUMIDITY Low
CARE Easy
HEIGHT & SPREAD 12 x 12in
(30 x 30cm)
WARNING! All parts are toxic to pets

The purple or variegated leaves of this highly decorative plant resemble those of shamrock. The triangular leaves also perform a party trick, folding up at night and opening during the day. In addition to the foliage, sprays of small pink or white starry flowers appear over many weeks from spring to summer.

WATERING Allow the top of the potting soil to dry out between waterings. From fall to winter, when the plant becomes dormant and the foliage starts to die off, refrain from watering. The plant may look dead, but if you then start watering again after 4–6 weeks, new leafy growth will soon reappear.

FEEDING Apply a balanced liquid fertilizer every month when the plant is in growth from spring to late summer. Stop feeding during dormancy.

PLANTING AND CARE Plant the bulbs in fall in a 6–8in (15–20cm) pot in an equal mix of aerated potting soil, multipurpose potting soil, and horticultural hard sand. The bulbs should be 2in (5cm) below the soil surface. False shamrock is also frequently sold in leaf as a potted plant. Set in a medium-light spot, out of direct sun, from spring to fall, and then move to a cool room in winter.

CALLA LILY
Zantedeschia species

TEMPERATURE 50–68°F (10–20°C)
LIGHT Bright indirect
HUMIDITY Moderate
CARE Average
HEIGHT & SPREAD Up to 2 x 2ft
(60 x 60cm)
WARNING! All parts are toxic

While the white arum lily (*Zantedeschia aethiopica*) is best grown outdoors, the smaller, often more colorful calla lilies, such as *Z. elliottiana* and *Z. rehmannii*, make beautiful houseplants. They feature plain or spotted leaves and the flowers, which comprise yellow, pink, purple, dark red, or black spathes (petal-like sheaths) around a spike of tiny flowers, appear from spring to fall.

WATERING Keep the potting soil moist from late spring to late summer; the potting soil should be almost dry in winter.

FEEDING Apply a balanced liquid fertilizer every 2 weeks from spring until the flowers have faded.

PLANTING AND CARE In late winter, plant in a wide pot in multipurpose potting soil, with the rhizomes (large, oval bulbs) just showing above the surface, and the eyes (dark bumps) uppermost. Set in a warm spot in bright indirect light. Allow foliage to die down in fall. Repot in winter, and store in a cool place.

ORCHIDS

Prized for their exotic flowers, orchids come in a vast range of shapes and colors, and some also have scented blooms. The stars of any show, use one as a focal point in a bright room, or recreate their natural inclination to cling to trees by growing those with aerial roots on bark or a log (see pp.88–91). While some of these divas demand lots of attention, others—most notably the widely available moth orchids (*Phalaenopsis*)—will thrive without too much fuss.

SPIDER ORCHID
Brassia species

TEMPERATURE 55–75°F (12–24°C)
LIGHT Bright indirect
HUMIDITY High
CARE Average
HEIGHT & SPREAD Up to 3 x 3ft
(1 x 1m)

Like colorful spiders crawling along arching stems, the unusual blooms of this orchid comprise long, thin, yellow or green petals, with brown or maroon stripes or spots, attached to a rounded central lip. The spidery flowers also have a delicious spicy scent and appear in late spring and summer, while the pseudobulbs (swellings at the base of the stems) each produce two or three long, strap-shaped green leaves.

WATERING Allow the top of the potting soil to dry out between waterings in spring and summer. Partly submerge the pot in a tray of unsoftened water for half an hour, then leave to drain. In winter, the plant needs a rest and should be kept drier, watering just enough to prevent the pseudobulbs from shrinking. Mist the leaves daily from spring to late summer and stand the pot on a tray of wet pebbles, or install a room humidifier.

FEEDING Apply special orchid fertilizer with every other watering from midspring, when new growth emerges, to late summer.

PLANTING AND CARE Plant the spider orchid in a 4–8in (10–20cm) clear pot in special orchid potting medium (or a 6:1:1 mix of composted bark, perlite, and charcoal). Do not cover the aerial roots, which should be left exposed to the light. Set in a bright position, out of direct summer sun and away from drafts, and provide good ventilation. Cut the flower spike down to just above the first node after blooming, then place in lower light. The orchid likes to be cramped, so only repot when growth starts to suffer.

CYMBIDIUM
Cymbidium species and hybrids

TEMPERATURE 50–75°F (10–24°C)
LIGHT Bright indirect
HUMIDITY Moderate
CARE Average
HEIGHT & SPREAD 2 x 2ft (60 x 60cm) for miniatures, and 4 x 2½ft (1.2 x 0.75m) for standards

This free-flowering orchid will brighten up your home from late fall to spring, when few other plants are at their best. The stems of large blooms emerge from between strap-shaped green leaves, creating an explosion of color. The named hybrids are easier than the species, and there are two types to choose from: large "standards" that can grow up to 4ft (1.2m), and the smaller, more popular "miniatures," which are ideal for a windowsill.

WATERING In spring and summer, allow the top of the potting soil to dry out between waterings, and water from above with unsoftened water, making sure that any excess can drain away. Reduce watering to once every 2 weeks in winter. Place on a tray of wet pebbles.

FEEDING Apply a half-strength general liquid fertilizer with every third watering in spring, then switch to special orchid fertilizer throughout summer.

PLANTING AND CARE Plant in a 6–8in (15–20cm) opaque pot in special orchid potting medium (or a 6:1:1 mix of composted bark, perlite, and charcoal). This ground-dwelling orchid does not have aerial roots, and does not need a clear pot. Stand in bright light all year, out of direct summer sun. Ideally, set it on a partly shaded patio outdoors in summer and early fall (before the frosts), when plants need a distinct drop between day and night temperatures to form flower buds. In late fall, keep in a cool room, ideally below 59°F (15°C); bring into a slightly warmer room to flower. Repot every year or two in spring.

Cymbidium hybrid

Cymbidium miniature

Named hybrids are the most widely available and easy to care for. Choose from the huge range of flower colors, many with patterned or spotted petals.

Miniature cymbidiums are compact hybrids, ranging in height from 12–24in (30–60cm). Like all cymbidiums, they need a cool room to flower well.

NOBILE DENDROBIUM
Dendrobium nobile hybrids

TEMPERATURE 40–75°F (5–24°C)
LIGHT Bright indirect
HUMIDITY Moderate to high
CARE Difficult
HEIGHT & SPREAD 24 x 18in
(60 x 45cm)

Upright canelike stems of scented flowers appear from fall to early spring on this flamboyant orchid. Those with pink or white flowers are the most popular, but they come in a wide range of colors. Although this is one of the easier dendrobiums to grow, be prepared to pamper it, and do not worry if the plant loses some leaves in winter, as it is a semideciduous.

WATERING From spring to late summer, water once or twice a week in the morning using lukewarm unsoftened water (see *Brassia* watering method on p.110). Reduce watering to every 2 weeks in early fall to stimulate flower buds to form; in winter, do not water, but mist occasionally to prevent the pseudobulbs (swellings at the base of the plant) from shriveling. Set on a tray of wet pebbles from early spring to late summer.

FEEDING Apply a half-strength balanced liquid fertilizer every 2–3 weeks from spring to summer. In late summer, change to a half-strength high-potassium fertilizer for one month, then discontinue feeding until the following spring.

PLANTING AND CARE Plant this orchid in a 6–8in (15–20cm) clear pot in special orchid potting medium (or a 6:1:1 mix of composted bark, perlite, and charcoal). Grow in a bright spot, out of direct summer sun, and away from drafts. To bloom, this dendrobium needs a distinct difference between day and night temperatures, and it is best grown outside in semishade from summer to early fall (before the frosts). In winter when blooming, keep it in an unheated room with a nighttime temperature of about 50°F (10°C) or slightly lower. Repot every year in spring.

Dendrobium nobile 'Star Class Akatsuki'

This brightly colored orchid produces spikes of dazzling fuchsia-pink flowers with white and yellow centers.

Dendrobium nobile 'Star Class Apollon'

One of the popular clear white forms of nobile dendrobium, it forms tall spikes of small, long-lasting blooms.

PANSY ORCHID
Miltoniopsis hybrids

TEMPERATURE 54–80°F (12–27°C)
LIGHT Bright indirect/Medium
HUMIDITY High
CARE Average
HEIGHT & SPREAD 2 x 2ft (60 x 60cm)

Often labeled as Miltonia (hybrids of *Miltoniopsis*), this compact orchid produces large, fragrant blooms with distinctive pansylike markings on the face, hence its common name. The flowers can appear in spring or fall, depending on the hybrid.

WATERING In the summer, apply unsoftened water every day or two from above, giving the plant a good soaking, and then leave it to drain. In winter, reduce watering to once every 2–3 weeks. Set on a tray of wet pebbles and mist every few days.

FEEDING Apply special orchid fertilizer every 2 weeks, but flush the plant with plenty of unsoftened water once a month to prevent a build-up of salts.

PLANTING AND CARE Plant in a 6–8in (15–20cm) clear pot in special orchid potting medium (or a 6:1:1 mix of composted bark, perlite, and charcoal). The pansy orchid will be happy in medium light in summer; move closer to the window in winter. Avoid direct sun and drafts, and repot annually in spring.

BUTTERFLY ORCHID
Oncidium hybrids

TEMPERATURE 55–77°F (13–25°C)
LIGHT Bright indirect
HUMIDITY Moderate
CARE Average
HEIGHT & SPREAD Up to 2 x 2ft
(60 x 60cm)

The stems of this dainty orchid hold dozens of small flowers that look like butterflies or dancing ladies, creating a spectacular effect, usually in fall. The hybrids are relatively easy and can be mounted on bark or slate.

WATERING Apply unsoftened water when the top of the potting soil is slightly dry. In winter, water just once a month. Set on a tray of wet pebbles and mist every day or two.

FEEDING Apply special orchid fertilizer, diluted to one-quarter strength, with every second or third watering.

PLANTING AND CARE Grow on bark, or in a 5–6in (12.5–15cm) opaque pot in special orchid potting medium. It likes to be cramped, so repot only when the pot becomes too small for the new growth.

NELLY ISLER
× *Oncidopsis Nelly Isler* gx

TEMPERATURE 60–75°F (16–24°C)
LIGHT Bright indirect/Medium
HUMIDITY High
CARE Difficult
HEIGHT & SPREAD Up to 20 x 20in
(50 x 50cm)

This orchid hybrid is prized for its tall stems of bright red flowers with white spotted lips and a yellow eye. Blooms appear at any time of year, but most flower in fall, and they have an intense lemony fragrance.

WATERING Using unsoftened water, apply when the top of the potting soil is slightly dry (see watering method for *Brassia* on p.110). In winter, reduce watering slightly. Set on a tray of wet pebbles and mist every day or two.

FEEDING Apply a half-strength orchid fertilizer every 2 weeks year-round.

PLANTING AND CARE Grow in a 6–8in (15–20cm) clear pot in special orchid potting medium. Keep out of direct sun, in temperatures of 60–75°F (16–24°C). After flowering, trim the stems to just above the lowest node (bump on the stem) to encourage a second bloom. Repot every year or two in spring.

SLIPPER ORCHID
Paphiopedilum 'Maudiae Femma'

TEMPERATURE 63–77°F (17–25°C)
LIGHT Bright indirect/Medium
HUMIDITY Moderate
CARE Average
HEIGHT & SPREAD 12 x 8in
(30 x 20cm)

This orchid has great allure and features large showy flowers in a wide range of colors, with a distinctive slipperlike pouch that gives rise to its common name. The blooms generally appear for many weeks from winter to early summer, although some hybrids flower at other times, too. The long green or mottled leaves form a fan shape, and provide interest while the plant is not in flower. Named hybrids are easier than the species to look after.

WATERING Using unsoftened water, keep the potting soil moist from spring to fall, applying water once or twice a week (see *Brassia* watering method on p.110). Reduce watering in winter, but do not let the potting soil dry out completely. Set on a tray of wet pebbles to raise humidity levels, but do not mist, as this may lead to rotting.

FEEDING Apply special orchid fertilizer every 2–3 weeks from spring to fall; in winter, apply it at half-strength and at the same frequency.

PLANTING AND CARE Grow the slipper orchid in a 5–8in (15–20cm) opaque pot in special orchid potting medium (or a 4:1 mix of finely composted bark and perlite). This ground-dwelling orchid does not need a clear pot, as it produces no aerial roots. Grow in medium light in summer, out of direct sun, and in full light in winter. The plain green-leaved orchids like cool conditions; the more widely available mottle-leaved types need warmth, with a minimum of 63°F (17°C) at night. Repot annually after flowering in a slightly larger container, making sure new growth is not buried.

MOTH ORCHID
Phalaenopsis hybrids

TEMPERATURE 61–80°F (16–27°C)
LIGHT Bright indirect/Medium
HUMIDITY Moderate
CARE Easy
HEIGHT & SPREAD Up to 3 x 2ft
(90 x 60cm)

One of the most widely available and easiest orchids to grow, the moth orchid produces long arching stems topped with large round blooms in a huge range of colors, some with delicate patterning. The flowers can appear at any time of the year. There are also miniature hybrids for small spaces, and all types are happy in high daytime winter temperatures and will grow well in a centrally heated home.

WATERING Keep the potting soil moist at all times and apply water every 5–7 days in the morning (ideally, use softened water in hard-water areas). Reduce watering slightly in winter, but do not let the potting soil dry out completely.

Phalaenopsis hybrid

Many orchids are not named when you buy them, but the most widely available will be easy-care hybrids. Simply choose colors to suit your scheme, and team up matching hues.

Set on a tray of wet pebbles; mist the plants occasionally in the morning, which allows excess water to dry before the colder nights.

FEEDING Apply a special orchid fertilizer with each watering once a week, but flush through the plant with plain water and no fertilizer once a month to remove excess salts. Reduce feeding to once a month in winter.

PLANTING AND CARE Plant in a 4–6in (10–15cm) clear pot in special orchid potting medium (or a 6:1:1 mix of composted bark, perlite, and charcoal). Do not bury the aerial roots, which need to be exposed. Set in medium light in summer; bring closer to a bright window in winter. Avoid drafts and major temperature fluctuations; these orchids prefer warmth year-round. After flowering, cut the stem just above the lowest node (bump on stem) to encourage a second bloom. Repot every 2 years in a slightly larger container.

Phalaenopsis So Petit range

This group of miniature hybrid moth orchids comes in a range of colors, including pink, peach, and white, and they fit neatly onto a windowsill.

VANDA ORCHID
Vanda hybrids

TEMPERATURE 61–90°F (16–32°C)
LIGHT Bright indirect
HUMIDITY High
CARE Difficult
HEIGHT & SPREAD 4 x 2ft (1.2 x 0.6m)

This tropical orchid is demanding, but its large colorful blooms, often patterned and up to 6in (15cm) in diameter, make the effort worthwhile when they appear in spring and summer. Vandas need very high levels of humidity, and they are commonly grown in a vase or an open wire basket without potting soil.

WATERING Water every morning by plunging the roots into a bucket of lukewarm unsoftened water for 15 minutes until the roots go green, then drain; reduce to every 3–4 days in winter. Vandas demand high humidity and should be misted a few times a day; alternatively, install a humidifier.

FEEDING Mist the leaves and roots once a week with a ready-mixed orchid fertilizer spray. Apply every 2 months in winter.

PLANTING AND CARE Grow in a slatted basket or in a large clear vase with no potting soil. Set in a bright spot, out of direct summer sun, but in good light in winter. A heated, well-ventilated room or greenhouse is ideal. Lower nighttime temperatures in fall encourage flower buds to form. To repot, soak the roots and gently pull them away from the sides of the basket, then place the plant in its small basket into a larger basket; the roots will then grow on without disturbance.

CAMBRIA ORCHID
× *Vuylstekeara* Cambria gx 'Plush'

TEMPERATURE 50–75°F (10–24°C)
LIGHT Bright indirect
HUMIDITY High
CARE Difficult
HEIGHT & SPREAD Up to 20 x 14in (50 x 35cm)

While this beautiful hybrid orchid is not widely available, it is worth seeking out if you like a challenge. The rewards for your efforts are tall arched stems of large, dark red, fragrant flowers, with white spotted lips and a yellow eye. The long-lasting blooms appear at any time of year, but mostly in winter or spring.

WATERING Apply unsoftened water when the top of the potting soil is slightly dry (use the method described for *Brassia* on p.110) and water every 5–7 days from spring to fall, and every 7–10 days in winter. Set on a tray of wet pebbles and mist the leaves every day or two, or install a room humidifier.

FEEDING Apply a half-strength orchid fertilizer with every second or third watering year-round.

PLANTING AND CARE Grow in a 4–8in (10–20cm) clear pot in special orchid potting medium. To promote flowering, make sure there is a 10°F (6°C) drop in temperature at night. After flowering, trim back the stems to just above the lowest node (bump on stem) to encourage a second bloom of blooms. Repot only when the pseudobulbs (swellings at the base of the stems) fill the container completely.

OTHER FLOWERING PLANTS

While many houseplants produce flowers, some are grown specifically for their beautiful blooms, and can be used to inject seasonal color into a green leafy display. This selection includes plants that bloom at different times of the year, and some that even flower in the depths of winter.

FLOWERING MAPLE
Abutilon × hybridum

TEMPERATURE 54–75°F (12–24°C)
LIGHT Bright indirect
HUMIDITY Low
CARE Average
HEIGHT & SPREAD Up to 36 x 24in (90 x 60cm)

Dress up your home with this tall shrub's large bell-shaped flowers, which come in a variety of colors, including red, yellow, pink, and white. The maplelike green or variegated foliage provides a foil for long-lasting summer blooms.

WATERING Keep the potting soil moist from spring to fall; in winter, allow the top of the potting soil to dry out between waterings.

FEEDING Apply a balanced liquid fertilizer every 2 weeks between spring and fall, replacing it in summer with a high-potassium fertilizer.

PLANTING AND CARE Grow in an equal mix of multipurpose and aerated potting soils in a 8–12in (20–30cm) pot. Set in a bright position, and move in winter to a cooler room with daytime temperatures of 61–68°F (16–20°C). Trim back stems and pinch back the tips in spring to create a bushier, compact plant. Prune again in fall if necessary. Repot every 2 years.

ANTHURIUM
Anthurium andraeanum AGM

TEMPERATURE 61–75°F (16–24°C)
LIGHT Bright indirect
HUMIDITY Moderate
CARE Average
HEIGHT & SPREAD 18 x 12in
(45 x 30cm)

This top-performing houseplant sports dramatic, arrow-shaped, dark green leaves and elegant waxy flowers, which appear throughout the year. It is best displayed in a simple modern pot, and the blooms—which come in white, red, pink, salmon, bicolors, and dark hues—are made up of a tear-shaped spathe (leaflike sheath) and a long spadix (spike of tiny flowers). As well as its stylish good looks and obvious charm, the anthurium, or flamingo flower as it is sometimes known, is also quite easy to grow.

WATERING Keep the potting soil moist throughout the year; avoid overwatering, which may rot the roots. Set on a tray of wet pebbles.

FEEDING Apply a half-strength, high-potassium liquid fertilizer every 2 weeks from spring to summer.

PLANTING AND CARE Plant with the top of the root ball 1in (2.5cm) below the soil surface in a 5–8in (12.5–20cm) pot and an equal mix of multipurpose and aerated potting soils. Cover the root ball with moss to prevent it drying out. Stand in bright indirect light and keep at 61–75°F (16–24°C) all year round. Repot only when the plant has become root-bound.

Anthurium andraeanum—white form

Most anthurium species produce bright red flowers, but the cooler, sophisticated white forms are also very popular and widely available.

Anthurium andraeanum 'Black Queen'

The fashion for dark blooms has led breeders to produce flowers in a range of sultry single shades, from burgundy to near black, and moody bicolors.

ANGEL'S TRUMPET
Brugmansia × candida

TEMPERATURE 61–77°F (16–25°C)
LIGHT High/Bright indirect
HUMIDITY Moderate
CARE Average
HEIGHT & SPREAD 4 x 3ft
(1.2 x 1m)
WARNING! All parts are toxic

The knock-out evening fragrance and large, showy, trumpet-shaped flowers of this tall plant make it a favorite for a big, bright room. The blooms come in yellow, pink, white, or red, but the plant has one major vice—all parts are toxic, so it is not a good choice for those with children or pets. You may also see it sold as *Datura*.

WATERING Keep the potting soil moist from spring to early fall; reduce watering so that the potting soil is barely moist in winter, when temperatures are lower.

FEEDING Apply a balanced liquid fertilizer every month in spring; switch to a high-potassium fertilizer in summer.

PLANTING AND CARE Grow in a 8–12in (20–30cm) pot in aerated potting soil. Set in a sunny spot and a cool room in winter. Wearing gloves, trim the stems after flowering to keep it compact, but do not prune too vigorously or you may lose the flowers. Repot every 2–3 years.

LISIANTHUS
Eustoma grandiflorum

TEMPERATURE 54–75°F (12–24°C)
LIGHT High/Bright indirect
HUMIDITY Low
CARE Average
HEIGHT & SPREAD 12 x 18in
(30 x 45cm)

The cup-shaped blooms of this pretty annual are often used in floral design, but the plant can also be grown as a houseplant, adding temporary color to a mixed display in spring and summer. The flowers are available in a wide range of colors, including purple, pink, white, and bicolors. Look out for compact varieties, which are sometimes sold as garden bedding plants.

WATERING Keep the soil moist from spring to fall, but avoid overwatering.

FEEDING From spring to fall, apply a high-potassium fertilizer every 2 weeks.

PLANTING AND CARE Plant lisianthus in a container about 6–8in (15–20cm) wide in multipurpose potting soil. Young plants bought in spring will grow rapidly if set in a sunny position, protected from strong midday sun in summer. Pinch back the tips of the stems in spring to create a bushier plant with more flowers, and deadhead faded blooms regularly. Buy new plants each year.

PERSIAN VIOLET
Exacum affine AGM

TEMPERATURE 65–75°F (18–24°C)
LIGHT Bright indirect
HUMIDITY Moderate to high
CARE Average
HEIGHT & SPREAD 8 x 8in (20 x 20cm)

This plant may only perform for a few months, but its fragrant, violet-blue flowers with yellow centers, which appear over many weeks above a mound of glossy green leaves, make it well worth growing. It is a biennial, which means it produces leaves in the first year and blooms in the second, but those you buy will flower the same year.

WATERING Keep the potting soil moist—the flowers fade quickly if the roots are dry. Set on a tray of wet pebbles to increase humidity.

FEEDING Apply a half-strength balanced liquid fertilizer every 2 weeks from spring to late summer.

PLANTING AND CARE You will probably not need to repot the plants, but if yours is root-bound (see pp.192–93), transfer it to a slightly larger pot of multipurpose potting soil. Try growing it from seed in winter or early spring (see pp.208–09).

GARDENIA
Gardenia jasminoides AGM

TEMPERATURE 61–75°F (16–24°C)
LIGHT Bright indirect
HUMIDITY High
CARE Difficult
HEIGHT & SPREAD 2 x 2ft (60 x 60cm)
WARNING! All parts are toxic to pets

This shrub's main appeal is its large, round, sweetly scented white flowers, which appear in summer and fall against a backdrop of glossy, dark green leaves. It can grow into a large plant in warm, frost-free climes but rarely reaches more than 2ft (60cm) tall when grown indoors in a pot.

WATERING From spring to fall, water with lukewarm unsoftened water, keeping the potting soil moist. In winter, allow the top of the potting soil to dry out between waterings. Maintain high humidity for the plant; stand on a tray of wet pebbles to increase humidity.

FEEDING From spring to late summer, apply a half-strength fertilizer designed for acid-loving plants every 2 weeks.

PLANTING AND CARE Grow gardenia in a 8–12in (20–30cm) pot in acidifying potting soil. Place in a bright spot, out of direct sunlight and drafts. To prevent the buds failing, it needs temperatures of 70–75°F (21–24°C) by day and 61–65°F (16–18°C) at night in summer. In winter, move to a sunny window. Repot every 2–3 years in spring.

WATERING Keep the potting soil moist from spring to fall; allow the top of the potting soil to dry out between waterings through winter.

FEEDING Apply a balanced liquid fertilizer once a month from spring to summer, then switch to a high-potassium fertilizer when the flower buds appear.

PLANTING AND CARE Plant in a large 8–12in (20–30cm) pot in a 3:1 mix of aerated potting soil and hard sand. In spring, set in a sunny room, but move to a cooler spot in winter after it has lost its leaves. Fruits will only ripen if temperatures are at least 55–60°F (13–16°C). Prune in spring, and repot every 2–3 years.

AZALEA
Rhododendron simsii

TEMPERATURE 50–75°F (10–24°C)
LIGHT Medium
HUMIDITY Low
CARE Average
HEIGHT & SPREAD 18 x 18in (45 x 45cm)
WARNING! All parts are toxic

The perfect pick-me-up in spring, the azalea's blend of glossy, dark green leaves and early blooms will liven up any cool room at this time of year. Its clusters of single or double flowers, sometimes with ruffled petals, come in shades of pink, red, white, or bicolors. The buds are beautiful, too, and the blooms last for many weeks.

WATERING Water with unsoftened water and keep the potting soil moist from early spring to fall; reduce watering just slightly over winter, but never let the plant dry out.

FEEDING Apply a balanced liquid fertilizer designed for acid-loving plants once a month from spring to fall.

PLANTING AND CARE Grow in a 6–8in (15–20cm) pot, depending on the size of the azalea, in acidifying potting soil. Set in medium light and a cool room when in flower. Stand the plant outside in shade or in a cool room in summer. Repot every 2–3 years in spring when root-bound.

AFRICAN VIOLET
Saintpaulia cultivars

TEMPERATURE 61–75°F (16–24°C)
LIGHT Bright indirect
HUMIDITY Moderate
CARE Average
HEIGHT & SPREAD Up to 4 x 8in (7.5 x 20cm)

This classic houseplant used to be found in almost every home, and it is now enjoying a renewed popularity. The small round flowers come in a wide variety of colors, including pink, red, purple, and white, and the petals may also be ruffled or frilly. African violets bloom throughout the year, the flowers appearing above soft, round, dark green leaves, which can be maroon beneath.

WATERING Water from below by placing the pot in a shallow tray of water for about 20 minutes, then leaving it to drain; soggy potting soil can lead to root rot. Allow the top of the potting soil to dry out between waterings. Set on a tray of wet pebbles to increase humidity.

FEEDING Apply a balanced liquid fertilizer once a month between spring and late summer.

PLANTING AND CARE Plant in a small 3–4in (7.5–10cm) pot in houseplant potting soil (or a 2:1 mix of aerated and multipurpose potting soils). Set in indirect light, out of drafts, but move to a sunny windowsill in winter. Deadhead regularly. Repot only when tightly root-bound.

JERUSALEM CHERRY
Solanum pseudocapsicum

TEMPERATURE 50–70°F (10–21°C)
LIGHT Bright indirect
HUMIDITY Low
CARE Average
HEIGHT & SPREAD 18 x 24in
(45 x 60cm)
WARNING! All parts are toxic

Unremarkable for much of the year, this plant explodes with color in fall and winter, when its red tomatolike fruits emerge, adding a colorful natural feature to winter festive decorations. The dark green, wavy-edged leaves and starry white summer flowers provide interest at other times. Do not eat the poisonous fruits.

WATERING Keep the potting soil moist from late spring to midwinter. After the fruits have faded, allow the top of the potting soil to dry out between waterings.

FEEDING Apply a balanced fertilizer once a month from late spring until the fruits appear. After fruiting, allow a few weeks without fertilizer.

PLANTING AND CARE Grow this plant in a 4–6in (10–15cm) pot, or larger, in an equal mix of aerated and multipurpose potting soils. Set in a bright spot from fall to spring. Stand it outside after the frosts or place in a cool bright room in summer. When the fruits have shriveled, cut the stems back by half to encourage bushy growth. Repot every 2–3 years in spring.

PEACE LILY
Spathiphyllum wallisii

TEMPERATURE 55–75°F (12–24°C)
LIGHT Bright indirect/Medium
HUMIDITY Moderate
CARE Easy
HEIGHT & SPREAD 24 x 24in
(60 x 60cm)
WARNING! All parts are toxic

The peace lily makes an elegant houseplant with its glossy dark green leaves and white flowers. The blooms are composed of a spike of small flowers, known as a spadix, and a tear-shaped spathe (petal-like sheath). The long-lasting blooms appear in spring and fade gradually from white to green. This plant also helps to reduce air pollutants.

WATERING From spring to fall, keep the potting soil moist; allow the top of the potting soil to dry out between waterings in winter. Set on a tray of wet pebbles to increase the humidity.

FEEDING Apply a balanced liquid fertilizer every 2 weeks from early spring to late fall.

PLANTING AND CARE Grow a peace lily in a 6–8in (15–20cm) pot in an equal mix of multipurpose and aerated potting soils. Stand in a bright spot or some shade, out of direct sun. Remove flower stems after blooming. Repot only when root-bound.

BIRD OF PARADISE
Strelitzia reginae

TEMPERATURE 55–75°F (12–24°C)
LIGHT High/Bright indirect
HUMIDITY High
CARE Difficult
HEIGHT & SPREAD 3 x 2ft (90 x 60cm)
WARNING! All parts are toxic

Large, blue-gray, paddle-shaped leaves provide a foil for this plant's sculptural flowers. While this plant takes a long time to flower indoors, doing so only when fully mature and well cared for, its gorgeous tropical blooms are worth the wait.

WATERING Keep the potting soil moist in spring and summer; reduce in fall and winter, allowing the top to dry out between waterings. Set on a tray of wet pebbles or use a humidifier.

FEEDING Apply a balanced liquid fertilizer every 2 weeks from spring to fall.

PLANTING AND CARE Grow in a 8–12in (20–30cm) pot in a 3:1 mix of aerated potting soil and hard sand. Set in high light and provide good ventilation in summer. Replace the top potting soil layer annually; repot every 2 years in spring.

CAPE PRIMROSE
Streptocarpus hybrids

TEMPERATURE 55–75°F (12–24°C)
LIGHT Bright indirect/Medium
HUMIDITY Moderate
CARE Easy
HEIGHT & SPREAD 24 x 24in
(60 x 60cm)

These free-flowering plants come in a huge assortment of colors to suit any decor or display, from white, pink, and red, to blues and purples. Many are also bicolored or have patterned petals. The blooms appear from spring to fall on slim stems above a rosette of wrinkled, lance-shaped green leaves, although some types, such as Crystal varieties, flower in winter, too. Cape primroses are quite easy to grow, and will decorate a windowsill or bright area of your home for many years.

WATERING Water either from above or below by placing the pot in a tray of water for 20 minutes and then leaving the plant to drain. Allow the top of the potting soil to dry out between waterings from spring to fall, and reduce so that the potting soil is almost dry in winter. Overwatering can cause root rot.

FEEDING Apply a high-potassium fertilizer once a month from spring to fall.

PLANTING AND CARE Plant in a small 4–6in (10–15cm) pot in multipurpose or houseplant potting soil. Set in a partly shaded spot, such as near a window that receives sun for half the day. During winter, move it to a window that receives direct sunlight for most of the day. Cut off flower stems as blooms begin to fade, and remove old leaves in spring when fresh growth appears. Repot in a slightly larger container each spring, but keep the plant a little root-bound.

Streptocarpus 'Polka-Dot Purple' AGM

One of the more unusual varieties, 'Polka-Dot Purple' sports white blooms, decorated with a fine purple lacy pattern that makes them looks spotted from a distance.

Streptocarpus 'Falling Stars' AGM

This award-winning pale blue Cape primrose produces an abundance of small blooms from early spring, and continues to flower until fall.

Streptocarpus 'Pink Leyla' AGM

The blooms of 'Pink Leyla' warrant close inspection to appreciate the clear white upper petals with delicate rose-pink brush strokes on the lower lips.

Streptocarpus 'Targa'

You may also find this Cape primrose under the name 'Stella', but either way, it is an excellent variety, producing a wealth of velvety-looking flowers with a slight sheen in two rich tones of purple.

FERNS

With their graceful, arching stems of finely divided or wavy-edged leaves, known as fronds, ferns make beautiful houseplants for low-light areas. Try using one as an elegant focal point on a table or stand, or group a few together to create a lush woodland effect. Ferns do not bear flowers or seeds, instead reproducing via spores held in small brown cases ("sporangia") on the undersides of the fronds.

DELTA MAIDENHAIR FERN
Adiantum raddianum AGM

TEMPERATURE 50-75°F (10-24°C)
LIGHT Bright indirect/Medium
HUMIDITY Moderate to high
CARE Average
HEIGHT & SPREAD 20 x 32in (50 x 80cm)

This elegant fern's dark stems and small round leaves produce an airy, treelike shape, and it makes a standout center-piece on a table or plant stand. It is a good candidate for a terrarium, too, as it thrives in humid conditions.

WATERING Keep the potting soil moist, not wet, at all times, and set on a tray of wet pebbles.

FEEDING Apply a half-strength balanced liquid fertilizer every 2 weeks from late fall to early spring.

PLANTING AND CARE Plant this fern in a 6-8in (15-20cm) container in multipurpose potting soil. Stand in medium light, out of direct sun and drafts, in an area of your home or office. Repot every 2 years in spring. If the plant starts to look worn, cut off all the stems at the base in spring; it will soon regenerate healthy growth.

BIRD'S NEST FERN
Asplenium nidus AGM

TEMPERATURE 55–75°F (13–24°C)
LIGHT Bright indirect/Medium
HUMIDITY Moderate to high
CARE Average
HEIGHT & SPREAD Up to 24 x 16in (60 x 40cm)

Unlike many ferns, this one has wide strap-shaped, undivided fronds. The handsome bright green foliage forms a compact vase shape, and some types, such as 'Crispy Wave', have crinkled, wavy-edged leaves that look like the ruffles on a flamenco skirt.

WATERING Keep the potting soil moist at all times, ensuring water does not drip into the frond rosette, which can lead to rotting. Set on a tray of wet pebbles.

FEEDING From spring to early fall, apply a half-strength balanced liquid fertilizer every 2 weeks.

PLANTING AND CARE Plant in an equal mix of charcoal, loam-based potting soil, and multipurpose potting soil, in a 6–8in (15–20cm) pot. Set in a draught-free area, out of direct sunlight, in an area of your home or office. Repot young plants every 2 years in spring.

FOXTAIL FERN
Asparagus densiflorus

TEMPERATURE 55–75°F (13–24°C)
LIGHT Bright indirect/Medium
HUMIDITY Low to moderate
CARE Easy
HEIGHT & SPREAD 2 x 2ft (60 x 60cm)

Despite its delicate appearance, the foxtail fern is very easy to grow and makes a handsome specimen in a hanging basket or tall pot, where its feathery fronds will cascade over the sides. Although not a true fern, its finely divided foliage and general appearance means it is usually sold as one.

WATERING Keep the potting soil moist from spring to fall; reduce in winter, allowing the top to dry out between waterings. It is tolerant of drier air than true ferns, but misting the foliage occasionally keeps it healthy.

FEEDING Apply a half-strength balanced liquid fertilizer once a month from spring to fall.

PLANTING AND CARE Plant in a small to medium-sized 4–6in (10–15cm) pot in quick-draining aerated potting soil, and set in bright indirect or medium light. Remove brown or overly long stems in spring, and, if root-bound, repot into a container one size larger.

RABBIT'S FOOT FERN
Davillia fejeensis

TEMPERATURE 55–75°F (13–24°C)
LIGHT Medium
HUMIDITY Moderate to high
CARE Average
HEIGHT & SPREAD 12 x 20in
(30 x 50cm)

Also known as the spider fern, its long, furry rhizomes (rootlike structures) make an eye-catching feature when they trail over the sides of a pot. You can also show them off in kokedama displays (see pp.76–79). The rich green lacy foliage adds to this plant's charms.

WATERING Keep the potting soil moist from spring to fall; allow the top of the potting soil to dry out between waterings in winter. Place on a tray of wet pebbles.

FEEDING Apply a half-strength balanced liquid fertilizer every 2 weeks from spring to early fall.

PLANTING AND CARE Plant in an equal mix of multipurpose and acidifying potting soils in a 6–8in (15–20cm) pot or a hanging basket. Do not bury the furry rhizomes. Place in an area of high humidity in medium light and a cool spot in summer in your home or office. Repot in spring if the plant becomes root-bound.

CROCODILE FERN
Microsorum musifolium 'Crocodyllus'

TEMPERATURE 55–75°F (13–24°C)
LIGHT Medium
HUMIDITY Moderate
CARE Average
HEIGHT & SPREAD
24 x 24in (60 x 60cm)

Display this remarkable-looking fern where its distinctive crocodile-skin leaf patterns can be admired up close—a hanging basket at eye level would be ideal. This architectural plant demands high humidity and will thrive in an area of your home or office where there is space for its wide-spreading fronds.

WATERING Water from spring to early fall when the top of the potting soil is almost dry; in winter, allow the top to dry out between waterings. Set on a tray of wet pebbles, and mist the leaves every few days in spring and summer.

FEEDING Apply a half-strength balanced liquid fertilizer once a month from spring to early fall.

PLANTING AND CARE In a 6–8in (15–20cm) pot, plant this fern in an equal mix of aerated and multipurpose potting soils. Place out of direct sunlight in a medium-light spot; it may need to be moved closer to a window in winter. Repot every 2 years or when root-bound.

BOSTON FERN
Nephrolepis exaltata AGM

TEMPERATURE 54–75°F (12–24°C)
LIGHT Bright indirect/Medium
HUMIDITY Medium
CARE Average
HEIGHT & SPREAD 24 x 24in
(60 x 60cm)

This popular plant, also known as the sword fern, is loved for its fountain of arching, finely divided, green fronds, which look spectacular flowing from a pot on a stand or a hanging basket. Relatively easy to care for, just maintain a humid atmosphere to prevent the leaves from turning brown.

WATERING From spring to fall, keep the potting soil moist, but not wet (fronds can rot in soggy potting soil); allow the top of the potting soil to dry out between waterings in winter. Place on a tray of wet pebbles.

FEEDING Apply a half-strength balanced liquid fertilizer once a month from spring to early fall.

PLANTING AND CARE Grow in a 5–6in (12.5–15cm) pot in a 50:50 mix of multipurpose and aerated potting soils, and place out of direct sunlight in bright or medium light. A room with good ventilation is an ideal home. Repot into a container one size larger every 2–3 years if the plant becomes root-bound.

BUTTON FERN
Pellaea rotundifolia AGM

TEMPERATURE 41–75°F (5–24°C)
LIGHT Bright indirect/Medium
HUMIDITY Medium
CARE Easy
HEIGHT & SPREAD 12 x 12in
(30 x 30cm)

The arching fronds of this graceful fern are composed of tiny button-shaped leaves that add a light, airy note to a display of foliage plants. It also makes an elegant subject for a small hanging basket, and can be used as edging for a large pot of taller shade-loving plants. Despite its delicate appearance, the button fern is easier to care for than many of its cousins, tolerating drier potting soil and lower humidity levels.

WATERING From spring to fall, water when the top of the potting soil feels almost dry; reduce watering slightly in winter. Stand on a tray of wet pebbles.

FEEDING Apply a half-strength balanced liquid fertilizer once a month year-round.

PLANTING AND CARE Grow in a 6in (15cm) pot, or one that fits the root ball, and plant in acidifying potting soil with a handful of perlite for added drainage. Place your fern in a bright- or medium-light area, out of direct sun—it will not suffer in drafts and is tolerant of low winter temperatures (not freezing). Repot in fresh potting soil every year or two, or when it becomes root-bound.

STAGHORN FERN
Platycerium bifurcatum AGM

TEMPERATURE 50–75°F (10–24°C)
LIGHT Bright indirect
HUMIDITY High
CARE Average
HEIGHT & SPREAD 12 x 36in
(30 x 90cm)

Impossible to overlook, the spectacular antler-shaped fronds of the staghorn fern make this demanding plant a popular choice. It actually produces two types of fronds: those at the base are round, flat, and green, and turn brown with age (so do not worry if this happens); the large, antler-shaped fronds grow from these smaller leaves.

WATERING Keep the potting soil moist from spring to early fall—set the pot in a tray of water for about 15 minutes if the round leaves have covered the potting soil, as soaking these can cause them to rot. Allow the top of the potting soil to dry out between waterings in winter. Mist the leaves every day in the morning and set on a tray of wet pebbles, or install a room humidifier.

FEEDING From spring to early fall, apply a balanced liquid fertilizer monthly.

PLANTING AND CARE Plant young ferns in a medium-sized 5–6in (12.5–15cm) pot or basket of orchid bark mixed with potting soil, and keep out of direct sunlight in a humid atmosphere. Repot every 2–3 years in spring.

CRETAN BRAKE FERN
Pteris cretica AGM

TEMPERATURE 55–75°F (13–75°C)
LIGHT Bright indirect/Medium
HUMIDITY Moderate
CARE Average
HEIGHT & SPREAD 2 x 2ft
(60 x 60cm)

This much-loved, dainty fern is best displayed on its own, where the wiry stems topped with slim, fingerlike fronds have space to expand. Choose between the plain green fronds of the species and variegated forms that feature a white stripe through the center of each leaflet.

WATERING Ensure the potting soil is moist, but not wet, from spring to fall; in winter, allow the top of the potting soil to dry out between waterings. Mist the foliage every day or two.

FEEDING Apply a half-strength balanced liquid fertilizer once a month from spring to early fall.

PLANTING AND CARE Plant this fern in a 5–6in (12.5–15cm) pot in a 2:1:1 mix of aerated potting soil, multipurpose potting soil, and charcoal. Set out of direct sunlight in a low-light spot and a humid atmosphere. Cut back brown or worn fronds at the base and repot every 2 years in spring.

PALMS

Transform your home into a tropical paradise with an elegant palm or palmlike plant, or include a few in a spacious office or bright room to evoke a parlor of the *Belle Époque* era when palms were first popular. Many of these tall, leafy plants are easy to grow, but check before buying if you are a beginner, as some are quite demanding. They are long-lived and will provide many years of beauty if given the right care.

PONYTAIL PALM
Beaucarnea recurvata AGM

TEMPERATURE 50–79°F (10–26°C)
LIGHT High/Bright indirect
HUMIDITY Low
CARE Easy
HEIGHT & SPREAD Up to 6 x 3ft (2 x 1m)

Native to Mexico, the ponytail palm's fountain of hairlike leaves and textured, distinctive trunk, with its large swollen base, make it a star attraction in any houseplant display. Although not officially a palm (it is a relative of the yucca), its similar features mean that it is often grouped with them.

WATERING In summer, water once a week, allowing the top of the potting soil to dry out between waterings; its bulbous stem stores water and will keep it alive if you forget occasionally. In winter, the potting soil should be almost dry.

FEEDING Apply a half-strength balanced liquid fertilizer once a month in spring and summer.

PLANTING AND CARE Grow your plant in a large 10–12in (25–30cm) pot in a 3:1 mix of aerated potting soil and sharp sand. Set in bright light. Replenish the top layer of potting soil every spring, and repot this slow-growing plant every 2–3 years in a container just one size larger.

PARLOR PALM
Chamaedorea elegans AGM

TEMPERATURE 50–80°F (10–27°C)
LIGHT Medium
HUMIDITY Low to moderate
CARE Easy
HEIGHT & SPREAD 4 x 2ft (1.2 x 0.6m)

While it doesn't have the yellow flowers that bloom on its outdoor form, this popular palm produces an elegant fountain of lush, feathery foliage. Happy in shade and tolerant of low levels of humidity, it is a very easy plant to grow and also helps to purify the air.

WATERING Allow the top of the potting soil to dry out between waterings in summer; reduce in winter so the potting soil is almost dry.

FEEDING Apply a balanced liquid fertilizer once a month from spring to fall.

PLANTING AND CARE Grow your palm in a large 8–12in (20–30cm) pot in an equal mix of aerated and multipurpose potting soils. Set in medium light; it will not be happy in deep shade. Cut out any brown fronds at the base; it is normal for fronds to die off from time to time. Repot every 2–3 years when root-bound.

FISHTAIL PALM
Caryota mitis

TEMPERATURE 55–75°F (13–24°C)
LIGHT Bright indirect
HUMIDITY Moderate to high
CARE Average
HEIGHT & SPREAD Up to 8 x 5ft (2.5 x 1.5m)
WARNING! All parts are toxic

The unusual triangular foliage of this palm makes it an intriguing houseplant. The fishtail-shaped, serrated leaves look like they have been torn or nibbled, while the stems fan out elegantly.

WATERING From spring to fall, water when the top of the potting soil feels just dry; reduce watering a little in winter. Stand on a tray of wet pebbles to increase the humidity.

FEEDING Apply a balanced liquid fertilizer monthly from spring to fall.

PLANTING AND CARE Grow in aerated potting soil in a pot that just fits the root ball (it likes to be constricted). Set in bright light, out of direct summer sun. Repot young plants every 2–3 years; replace the top layer of potting soil each spring when mature.

SAGO PALM
Cycas revoluta AGM

TEMPERATURE 55–75°F (13–24°C)
LIGHT Bright indirect
HUMIDITY Moderate
CARE Easy
HEIGHT & SPREAD 24 x 24in
(60 x 60cm)
WARNING! All parts are toxic

Although not a true palm, this chunky plant's textured trunk, topped with arching fronds, certainly looks like one. While it is, in fact, a cycad (an ancient group of slow-growing plants), it would not look out of place on a tropical beach. Beware the sharp, needlelike leaves when positioning it.

WATERING From spring to fall, allow the top of the potting soil to dry out a little before watering. In winter, the potting soil should be almost dry. Overwatering, or watering the crown (where the leaves emerge), can cause rot. Mist the leaves in summer.

FEEDING Apply a half-strength balanced liquid fertilizer once a month from spring to fall.

PLANTING AND CARE Grow in a 8–12in (20–30cm) pot in an equal mix of aerated and multipurpose potting soils. Set it in good light, out of direct summer sun, and away from heaters in winter. It is a slow-growing plant, and will need repotting every 3 years or when root-bound.

ARECA PALM
Dypsis lutescens AGM

TEMPERATURE 55–75°F (13–24°C)
LIGHT Bright indirect
HUMIDITY Moderate
CARE Average
HEIGHT & SPREAD 6 x 3ft (2 x 1m)

Also known as the butterfly palm, this bold and attractive houseplant has arching, wide, glossy green fronds that make it perfect as a framing accent or privacy screen. It is easy to grow, and is considered one of the best houseplants for removing air pollutants.

WATERING From spring to early fall, allow the top of the potting soil to dry out between waterings; reduce watering in winter so the potting soil is almost dry. Stand on a tray of wet pebbles to increase the humidity.

FEEDING Apply a half-strength balanced liquid fertilizer (not too salty) monthly during the growing season from spring to fall.

PLANTING AND CARE Grow in a 8–12in (20–30cm) pot in aerated potting soil. Set in indirect light, and away from heaters in winter. Remove dead fronds at the base, and repot every 3 years in spring if root-bound.

KENTIA PALM
Howea forsteriana AGM

TEMPERATURE 55–75°F (13–24°C)
LIGHT Medium
HUMIDITY Moderate
CARE Average
HEIGHT & SPREAD Up to 8 x 5ft
(3 x 2m)

Perfect for a shady room, the kentia palm has tall stems of dark green, glossy leaves that fan out elegantly to create a striking feature plant. Relatively easy to grow, it is a good choice for beginners.

WATERING Water from spring to fall when the top of the potting soil feels slightly dry; in winter, reduce so that the potting soil is barely moist. Stand on a tray of wet pebbles to increase the humidity.

FEEDING Apply a balanced liquid fertilizer every 2 weeks from spring to early fall.

PLANTING AND CARE Plant this palm in a 8–12in (20–30cm) pot in a 3:1 mix of aerated potting soil and sharp sand. Stand in medium light and away from drafts. Replace the top of the potting soil annually in spring, but repot only when the plant is tightly root-bound.

MINIATURE DATE PALM
Phoenix roebelenii AGM

TEMPERATURE 50–75°F (10–24°C)
LIGHT Bright indirect/Medium
HUMIDITY Moderate
CARE Average
HEIGHT & SPREAD 6 x 5ft (1.8 x 1.5m)

Like one of the classic palms along the Côte d'Azur, this plant's textured stem and fine, feathery fronds have a stylish elegance. Almost as wide as it is tall, it needs plenty of space to show off its sculptural silhouette. Mature plants bear cream summer flowers and edible fruits.

WATERING Keep the potting soil moist from spring to fall; in winter, allow the top to dry out between waterings. Stand on a tray of wet pebbles, and mist the leaves regularly in warm weather.

FEEDING Apply a balanced liquid fertilizer monthly from spring to fall.

PLANTING AND CARE Grow in a pot that just fits the root ball, in aerated potting soil. Stand in indirect light or a little shade, away from drafts. If possible, move to a cooler room in winter. Replace the top of the potting soil each spring; repot every 2–3 years when root-bound.

LADY PALM
Rhapis excelsa AGM

TEMPERATURE 50–77°F (10–25°C)
LIGHT Medium/Low
HUMIDITY Low to moderate
CARE Easy
HEIGHT & SPREAD Up to 6 x 6ft (2 x 2m)

If you are looking for a palm with a difference, try this unusual plant. Its bamboolike stems and large fronds, composed of blunt-ended, ribbed leaves, catch the eye when displayed in a large room or hallway. Slow-growing and tolerant of low-light conditions, it is one of the easiest palms to grow, making it ideal for a beginner. The smaller *Rhapis humilis* is another good choice.

WATERING Keep the potting soil moist from spring to fall, but avoid waterlogging. Reduce in winter so that the top of the potting soil feels dry between waterings. Mist the leaves every few days in summer.

FEEDING Apply a balanced liquid fertilizer 2–3 times during the growing season from spring to fall, or use a slow-release fertilizer once in early spring.

PLANTING AND CARE Grow in a pot that just fits the root ball in a 3:1 mix of multipurpose potting soil and perlite. Stand in medium light; it will tolerate deeper shade in summer but may need to be moved closer to the window in winter. Trim off old, brown fronds close to the trunk when they appear. Repot every 2–3 years, but only when root-bound.

TRAILING AND CLIMBING PLANTS

Cover your walls with flowers and foliage and inject color into the space above your head with these climbing and trailing plants. Some climbers can be grown up a mossy pole to keep them compact, or you can attach their twining stems to wires and trellises affixed to your walls. Easy to grow in hanging baskets or cascading from shelves, trailers are the perfect option when floor space is tight.

LIPSTICK PLANT
Aeschynanthus pulcher AGM

TEMPERATURE 65–80°F (18–27°C)
LIGHT Bright indirect
HUMIDITY Moderate
CARE Average
HEIGHT & SPREAD 8 x 28in (20 x 70cm)

Cascading stems of fleshy green leaves create a lush foliage effect all year round, but the show really starts in summer when this trailer's spectacular red tubular flowers open, emerging from darker cases (sepals) like bright lipsticks.

WATERING From spring to fall, apply lukewarm unsoftened water when the top of the potting soil feels dry. Keep it a little drier in winter.

FEEDING Use a half-strength balanced liquid fertilizer once a month in spring and summer.

PLANTING AND CARE Grow in a pot that just fits the root ball, in a 4:1:1 mix of aerated potting soil, sand, and perlite. Hang in bright light, out of direct sun, and keep warm year-round. Repot plants in spring when tightly root-bound.

BOUGAINVILLEA
Bougainvillea × buttiana

TEMPERATURE 50–79°F (10–26°C)
LIGHT High
HUMIDITY Low
CARE Average
HEIGHT & SPREAD Up to 5 x 5ft
(1.5 x 1.5m)
WARNING! All parts are toxic to pets

This climber will cover a wall in a sunny room with twining stems of small green leaves and bright flowers, or you can train it up canes or a hoop to keep it compact. The papery blooms comprise red, pink, or white bracts (petal-like modified leaves) and tiny cream flowers.

WATERING From spring to early fall, keep the potting soil moist; reduce watering in winter so the potting soil is barely moist.

FEEDING Apply a balanced liquid fertilizer every 2 weeks from spring to late summer, replacing it with a high-potassium fertilizer at every third application.

PLANTING AND CARE Grow in a pot that fits the root ball in aerated potting soil. Stand in high light, and tie the stems to canes, a hoop, or wires affixed to a wall. Prune sideshoots in fall. Repot young plants every 2 years; refresh the top layer of potting soil each spring when mature.

ROSARY VINE
Ceropegia linearis subsp. *woodii*

TEMPERATURE 46–75°F (8–24°C)
LIGHT High/Bright indirect
HUMIDITY Moderate
CARE Easy
HEIGHT & SPREAD 2 x 36in (5 x 90cm)

The threadlike stems of this plant's tiny heart-shaped leaves tumble over the sides of its pot in a gentle wave. Display it high enough for the plant's long stems to trail down to where you can admire the patterned leaves, which are gray-green with purple undersides. The small pink and purple tubular summer flowers are followed by long, needlelike seedpods.

WATERING Water only when the top of the potting soil feels dry; in winter, reduce watering so the potting soil is almost dry.

FEEDING Apply a half-strength balanced liquid fertilizer every 2 weeks in summer.

PLANTING AND CARE Grow in cactus potting soil in a 4–8in (10–20cm) pot. Hang your plant in a basket or set on a shelf in bright light; it may lose its coloration if the light levels are too low. Repot only when root-bound.

SPIDER PLANT
Chlorophytum comosum

TEMPERATURE 45–76°F (7–25°C)
LIGHT Bright indirect/Medium
HUMIDITY Low
CARE Easy
HEIGHT & SPREAD 1x 2ft (12 x 60cm)

Do not dismiss the spider plant just because it is widely available and easy to grow. It makes an eye-catching feature in a pot on a stand or in a hanging basket, its arching green and yellow leaves flowing gracefully over the sides, while baby plantlets dangle from long stems like spiders on silken threads.

WATERING Keep the potting soil moist from spring to fall, and allow the top to dry out between waterings in winter.

FEEDING From midspring to early fall during the growing season, apply a half-strength balanced liquid fertilizer monthly.

PLANTING AND REPOTTING Plant in a 50:50 mix of multipurpose and aerated potting soils in a pot that will accommodate the root ball. Set in bright or medium light, out of direct sun. It will tolerate gloomier areas but may not produce plantlets. Repot every 2–3 years in spring when the plant is root-bound.

GRAPE IVY
Cissus rhombifolia AGM

TEMPERATURE 59–75°F (12–24°C)
LIGHT Bright indirect/Medium
HUMIDITY Low
CARE Easy
HEIGHT & SPREAD Up to 6 x 6ft
(2 x 2m)

The glossy lobed foliage of this easy-care plant will trail from a basket or scramble up a trellis to cover the wall. The leaves have a silvery sheen when young, and then mature to dark green, giving a two-toned effect.

WATERING Keep the potting soil moist from spring to fall; reduce in winter so it is barely moist.

FEEDING Apply a balanced liquid fertilizer monthly from spring to fall.

PLANTING AND CARE Plant in aerated potting soil in a 6–8in (15–20cm) pot. If you grow it as a climber, tie the shoots in regularly to their supports. Trim back long growth in spring, and repot every 2–3 years or when root-bound, or replace the top layer of potting soil of mature plants each spring.

GOLDEN POTHOS
Epipremnum aureum AGM

TEMPERATURE 59–75°F (15–24°C)
LIGHT Bright indirect/Medium/Low
HUMIDITY Low
CARE Easy
HEIGHT & SPREAD Up to 6 x 6ft
(2 x 2m)
WARNING! All parts are toxic

One of the best houseplants for beginners, the almost indestructible golden pothos produces trailing or climbing stems of large heart-shaped leaves that create a lush tropical effect. Display it in a hanging basket or set the pot on a tall plant stand anywhere in your home, apart from areas in full sun.

WATERING Allow the top of the potting soil to dry out between waterings from spring to fall; in winter, keep barely moist.

FEEDING Apply a balanced liquid fertilizer monthly from spring to fall.

PLANTING AND CARE Plant in aerated potting soil in a pot that fits the root ball. Set in bright or low light, out of direct sun. If grown as a climber, tie stems to a moss pole, trellis, or wires. Prune in spring. Repot every 2 years; replace the top layer of potting soil of mature plants each spring.

CREEPING FIG
Ficus pumila 'Snowflake'

TEMPERATURE 55–75°F (13–24°C)
LIGHT Bright indirect/medium
HUMIDITY Low
CARE Average
HEIGHT & SPREAD Up to 3 x 3ft
(90 x 90cm)
WARNING! All parts are toxic to pets

Use this dainty little trailing plant to dress up a hanging basket or flow over the sides of a pot of flowering or larger foliage plants. It can also be persuaded to climb a trellis, creating a textured screen of small, round, cream-edged leaves. While fairly easy to grow, if the plant is not watered regularly and left to drain, the foliage can soon dry out.

WATERING Keep the potting soil moist at all times, but a little drier in winter. Mist every day or two in hot summer weather.

FEEDING Apply a balanced liquid fertilizer monthly in spring and summer.

PLANTING AND CARE Plant in a 4–8in (10–20cm) pot in aerated potting soil. Set in bright indirect or medium light. Pinch back the stem tips to produce bushy growth. If plants start to look leggy, cut them back vigorously to promote new leafy growth. Repot every 2 years in spring.

HOYA
Hoya species AGM

TEMPERATURE 61–75°F (16–24°C)
LIGHT Bright indirect
HUMIDITY Moderate
CARE Average
HEIGHT & SPREAD 13 x 13ft (4 x 4m)
WARNING! Leaves dangerous to pets

The waxy white flowers of this beautiful climber release a sweet fragrance when they open in summer. To cover a wall with long leafy stems, choose *Hoya carnosa*, or, if you have a small space to fill, opt for the more compact *Hoya lanceolata* subsp. *bella* AGM (above).

WATERING From spring to fall, keep the potting soil moist; water when the top of the potting soil is dry in winter. Set on a tray of wet pebbles to increase the humidity.

FEEDING Apply a half-strength high-potassium fertilizer every 2 weeks from spring to fall.

PLANTING AND CARE Plant in a pot that easily fits the root ball, in an equal mix of orchid potting medium, multipurpose potting soil, and perlite. Prune lightly in fall, but do not remove the flower stalks, as more blooms will grow from these stumps. Repot in spring when root-bound.

JASMINE
Jasminum polyanthum AGM

TEMPERATURE 50–75°F (10–24°C)
LIGHT Bright indirect
HUMIDITY Low
CARE Average
HEIGHT & SPREAD Up to 10 x 10ft
(3 x 3m)

When it flowers in midwinter, this climber's sweet scent will fill a cool room, such as a hallway, with fragrance. The blooms are pink in bud, and appear over many weeks between the dark green leaves. This is a large plant, and while you can train it up canes when young, it soon becomes a tangle of stems if not given space to expand on wires or a trellis.

WATERING Keep the potting soil moist from spring to late summer; reduce watering a little in winter, but ensure the soil is moist when in bud and flower.

FEEDING Apply a balanced liquid fertilizer every 2 weeks from spring to fall.

PLANTING AND CARE Plant in a pot that just fits the root ball in aerated potting soil, mixed with a few handfuls of perlite. Keep cool, as jasmine will suffer in warm, centrally heated rooms. Prune after flowering—you can be quite brutal to keep it compact. Only repot young plants; for mature plants, just replace the top layer of potting soil each spring.

MANDEVILLA
Mandevilla x *amoena* 'Alice du Pont' AGM

TEMPERATURE 59–75°F (15–24°C)
LIGHT Bright indirect
HUMIDITY Moderate
CARE Difficult
HEIGHT & SPREAD Up to 22 x 22ft
(7 x 7m)

It is easy to be tempted by the large, pink, tropical flowers of this twining climber, but remember that it needs a large space to thrive, and may sulk in the average living room. However, it makes an outstanding feature on a wall in a room with a skylight.

WATERING Keep the potting soil moist from spring to fall; reduce in winter so the potting soil is barely moist. Mist the foliage every day in summer.

FEEDING Apply a balanced liquid fertilizer once a month in spring, and switch to a high-potassium fertilizer in summer.

PLANTING AND CARE Grow in a large 10–12in (25–30cm) pot in a 3:1 mix of aerated potting soil and hard sand. Stand in bright light, out of direct summer sun. Prune in spring to create a framework of 3–5 strong shoots; if there is only one shoot, reduce it by a third to prompt more to form. Replace the top layer of soil annually in spring, rather than repotting.

SWISS CHEESE PLANT
Monstera deliciosa

TEMPERATURE 65–80°F (18–27°C)
LIGHT Bright indirect/Medium
HUMIDITY Moderate
CARE Easy
HEIGHT & SPREAD Up to 26 x 8ft
(8 x 2.5m)
WARNING! All parts are toxic

This classic climbing plant first became popular in the 1970s. Admired for its glossy, heart-shaped, lobed, and perforated leaves, which give rise to its name, this easy-care plant is often sold with the stems tied to a mossy pole.

WATERING Water when the top of the potting soil feels dry; reduce watering slightly in winter. Set on a tray of wet pebbles.

FEEDING Apply a half-strength balanced liquid fertilizer monthly from spring to fall.

PLANTING AND CARE Grow in a 8–12in (20–30cm) pot in a 3:1 mix of aerated potting soil and sand. Set in bright indirect or medium light; shaded foliage will not produce holes. Prune in spring, and wipe the leaves regularly to remove dust. Repot every 2–3 years, or replace the top layer of potting soil annually in spring.

RED PASSION FLOWER
Passiflora racemosa AGM

TEMPERATURE 54–75°F (12–24°C)
LIGHT Bright indirect
HUMIDITY Moderate
CARE Difficult
HEIGHT & SPREAD Up to 10 x 3ft (3 x 1m)

The most widely available passion flower is the blue form (*Passiflora caerulea*), which is hardy and easier to grow outside in mild regions, while this more unusual red type is tender. Its showy, bowl-shaped, summer flowers lend a tropical note to a bright room with a skylight. It also produces pale green edible fruits.

WATERING Keep the potting soil moist from spring to fall. In winter, water only when the top of the potting soil feels dry. Set on tray of wet pebbles to increase the humidity.

FEEDING Apply a balanced liquid fertilizer every 2 weeks from midspring to late summer.

PLANTING AND CARE Grow in a 8–12in (20–30cm) pot in aerated potting soil. Stand in bright indirect light, and prune in early spring. Repot young plants in spring; when mature, just replace the top layer of potting soil annually.

HEARTLEAF PHILODENDRON
Philodendron scandens AGM

TEMPERATURE 60–75°F (16–24°C)
LIGHT Bright indirect/Medium
HUMIDITY Low to moderate
CARE Easy
HEIGHT & SPREAD Up to 5 x 5ft
(1.5 x 1.5m)
WARNING! All parts are toxic

This impressive climber will cover a wall with its heart-shaped leaves, which can grow up to 10in (20cm) in length, transforming a living room into a lush jungle in no time. It is easy to care for, grows well in low light, and can be trained up a mossy pole to keep it compact in a small space.

WATERING Keep the potting soil moist from spring to fall; reduce in winter, watering only when the top of the potting soil feels dry. Maintain low to moderate humidity for the plant.

FEEDING Apply a balanced liquid fertilizer once a month from spring to early fall.

PLANTING AND CARE Plant in a 6in (15cm) pot in a 2:1 mix of aerated potting soil and sand or perlite. Young plants can be grown in a hanging basket, with the stems trailing down. As they grow larger, attach the stems to a mossy pole, a trellis, or horizontal wires affixed to a wall. Stand in bright indirect or medium light; it tolerates darker shade but may not grow as vigorously. Wipe leaves regularly to remove dust. Prune in late winter and repot when roots have filled the existing pot, or replace the top layer of compost annually.

CAPE IVY
Senecio macroglossus 'Variegatus' AGM

TEMPERATURE 50–77°F (10–25°C)
LIGHT High/Bright indirect in summer
HUMIDITY Low
CARE Easy
HEIGHT & SPREAD Up to 5 x 5ft
(1.5 x 1.5m)
WARNING! All parts are toxic

Masquerading as a regular ivy, this beautiful houseplant has a little more class, with its glossy, fleshy, green and yellow leaves and dark twining stems. Use it to trail from a basket, or grow it on a hoop or up a tripod or trellis.

WATERING Allow the top of the potting soil to dry out between waterings from spring to late summer; reduce watering in fall and winter so it is barely moist.

FEEDING Apply a half-strength balanced liquid fertilizer from spring to fall.

PLANTING AND CARE Plant Cape ivy in a 6in (15cm) pot in cactus potting soil or a 3:1 mix of aerated potting soil and sharp sand. Stand in direct sun, moving to bright indirect light in midsummer. Trim the shoot tips in spring if they get too long, and tie the stems to their support regularly. Repot every 2–3 years or when the plant becomes root-bound.

STRING OF PEARLS
Senecio rowleyanus

TEMPERATURE 50–77°F (10–25°C)
LIGHT High/Bright indirect in summer
HUMIDITY Low
CARE Easy
HEIGHT & SPREAD 2 x 36in (5 x 90cm)
WARNING! All parts are toxic

The slender stems of little pealike leaves flow from this trailing plant's pot like strings of green pearls, making an intriguing feature. It is a good choice for beginners, since the fleshy "beads" retain moisture and will sail through periods of neglect. Small white tubular flowers may also appear in spring.

WATERING Allow the top of the potting soil to dry out between waterings from spring to fall; in winter, keep barely moist so the beads do not shrivel up.

FEEDING Apply a half-strength balanced liquid fertilizer from spring to fall.

PLANTING AND CARE Plant in cactus potting soil or a 3:1 mix of aerated potting soil and sharp sand, in a 4–6in (10–15cm) pot. Set in indirect light in summer and a cooler but bright spot in winter. Trim in spring and repot every 2–3 years.

BABY'S TEARS
Soleirolia soleirolii

TEMPERATURE 23–75°F (-5–24°C)
LIGHT Bright indirect/Medium
HUMIDITY Moderate
CARE Easy
HEIGHT & SPREAD 2 x 36in (5 x 90cm)

This pretty plant forms a mound of tiny leaves on wiry stems, which looks like a mop of curly hair trailing daintily from its pot. It suits contemporary displays, flowing from the top of three identical tall pots. Take care when planting it up with partners; it is fast-growing and can take over if not trimmed regularly. Tiny pink-white flowers appear in summer.

WATERING Keep the potting soil moist from spring to fall, and slightly drier in winter. If left to dry out, the leaves will shrivel and die.

FEEDING Apply a half-strength balanced liquid fertilizer every month from spring to fall.

PLANTING AND CARE Plant this trailer in a 4–6in (10–15cm) pot in a 3:1 mix of aerated potting soil and hard sand. Display in bright or medium light, out of direct sun. Trim the stem tips to maintain bushy growth. Repot when the plant becomes root-bound.

STEPHANOTIS
Stephanotis floribunda AGM

TEMPERATURE 50–73°F (10–23°C)
LIGHT Bright indirect
HUMIDITY Moderate
CARE Average
HEIGHT & SPREAD Up to 10 x 10ft
(3 x 3m)

This climber's long, twining stems of glossy green leaves and fragrant, long-lasting, waxy white flowers combine to create a spectacular visual and sensory effect in summer. Given a large pot and good care, it can be grown along wires to cover a wall, or train it over a large hoop or on a trellis and prune the stems regularly to keep it more compact.

WATERING Keep the potting soil moist from spring to fall; allow the top to dry out between waterings in winter. Stand on a tray of wet pebbles and mist the leaves every day or two in summer.

FEEDING Apply a high-potassium liquid fertilizer every 2 weeks from spring to fall.

PLANTING AND CARE Grow in a pot that fits the root ball in aerated potting soil. Set in bright indirect light, out of direct sun. Keep plants cool in summer—around 70–73°F (21–23°C) is ideal—and a little cooler still (but not cold) in winter. Trim back lightly in spring, and replace large, overgrown plants. Repot every 2–3 years or renew the top layer of potting soil each spring.

SILVER-INCH PLANT
Tradescantia zebrina AGM

TEMPERATURE 54–75°F (12–24°C)
LIGHT Bright indirect
HUMIDITY Low to moderate
CARE Easy
HEIGHT & SPREAD Up to 6 x 24in
(15 x 60cm)

The gently trailing stems of the silver-inch plant make a striking feature in a hanging basket or pot on a shelf in a bright room. The fleshy silver and green striped leaves are purple when young, and the undersides remain purple as they mature, creating a colorful three-toned effect. Small pinkish-purple flowers appear throughout the year.

WATERING From spring to fall, water when the top of the potting soil is almost dry; in winter, reduce so that the potting soil is barely moist. Maintain low to moderate humidity for the plant.

FEEDING Apply a balanced liquid fertilizer once a month from spring to early fall.

PLANTING AND CARE Grow in a 3:1 mix of aerated potting soil and sharp sand or perlite and a 6–8in (15–20cm) pot. In summer, stand in bright light, out of direct sun. Trim the stem tips in spring to maintain bushy growth. Repot every 2–3 years or when root-bound.

CARNIVOROUS PLANTS

These fascinating plants make intriguing houseplants. They have developed a range of colorful pitchers or sticky leaves and stems to trap and consume insects and other small creatures, which provide them with essential nutrients. Most need too-wet soil to thrive, and some require special care, so check that you can provide the conditions they need.

CALIFORNIA PITCHER PLANT
Darlingtonia californica AGM

TEMPERATURE 45–75°F (7–24°C)
LIGHT High
HUMIDITY Moderate
CARE Difficult
HEIGHT & SPREAD 14 x 8in
(40 x 20cm)

Also known as the cobra lily, the pitchers of this unusual plant are hooded and feature fanglike structures that resemble a snake's head. Purple-veined flowers appear in spring, followed by red-veined pitchers that emit a honey scent to attract their prey. This plant is quite demanding, so ensure you can offer the exacting conditions it needs.

WATERING Water your plant daily with unsoftened water, or set in a shallow water-filled tray.

FEEDING Do not feed this pitcher plant.

PLANTING AND CARE Plant in an equal mix of sphagnum moss, perlite, and horticultural sand (potting soil will kill this plant). Set in sun during the summer. When dormant in winter, place the plant outside in a sheltered area or in a cold, bright, unheated room. You may see tiny insects if you look into the pitchers. These little creatures live inside the plant and eat other prey that fall in; the pitcher then digests their feces.

CAPE SUNDEW
Drosera capensis

TEMPERATURE 45–85°F (7–29°C)
LIGHT High/Bright indirect
HUMIDITY Moderate
CARE Easy
HEIGHT & SPREAD 6 x 8in (15 x 20cm)

The easiest sundew to grow, this plant's long slim leaves are covered with colorful tentacles that produce a sticky mucus that looks like drops of water (hence the name). The leaves ensnare insects and then curl around their trapped prey, which is then slowly absorbed by the plant. In late spring or early summer, pink flowers appear that last just 1 day—opening in the morning, then closing in the afternoon.

WATERING Set the pot in a deep tray of unsoftened water. In its natural habitat, the plant is dormant in winter and requires less water, but in a warm home, leave it in its water tray to continue growing throughout the year.

FEEDING Do not feed Cape sundews.

PLANTING AND CARE Plant in a tall 4–6in (10–15cm) pot in an equal mix of sphagnum moss and perlite; potting soil will kill the plant. Set in a bright spot and open windows regularly to allow insects in. These will be attracted to the plant, which needs just 2–3 per month to survive. Remove dead leaves and repot annually in fresh growing medium. Remove flowers to prevent self-seeding.

MONKEY CUPS
Nepenthes hybrids

TEMPERATURE 45–80°F (7–27°C)
LIGHT Bright indirect
HUMIDITY Moderate to high
CARE Average
HEIGHT & SPREAD Up to 12 x 18in (30 x 45cm)

The dark red pitchers that dangle from slender stems of this unusual tropical plant look otherworldly, emerging from the tips of spear-shaped green leaves. The pitchers' color and nectar attracts insects, which drown when they fall in.

WATERING Never stand in a tray of water, but keep the potting soil moist. Water from above with unsoftened water. Set on a tray of wet pebbles.

FEEDING Apply a premixed foliar fertilizer spray to the leaves every 2 weeks. You can give it an occasional fresh fly or insect, although this is rarely needed.

PLANTING AND CARE Plant in a pot or hanging basket using a mix of chopped bark, sphagnum moss, and perlite from a carnivorous plant supplier; potting soil will kill the plant. Set in a bright spot out of direct sun with good ventilation. Repot every 2–3 years when root-bound.

VENUS FLY TRAP
Dionaea muscipula

TEMPERATURE 40–95°F (4–35°C)
LIGHT High
HUMIDITY Moderate
CARE Average
HEIGHT & SPREAD Up to 4 x 8in (10 x 20cm)

This plant's snapping jawlike leaves trap flying insects that come within reach, but it will soon die if coaxed to perform this trick too often. It has two types of leaves: the spring foliage is broader and produces traps close to the center of the plant, while the summer leaves are longer and develop red-tinged traps farther away. White tubular flowers appear in spring.

WATERING Place the pot in a deep tray of unsoftened water from spring to late summer; from fall to late winter, when dormant, remove it from the tray but keep the growing medium moist.

FEEDING Do not feed Venus fly traps.

PLANTING AND CARE Plant in a 4–6in (10–15cm) pot, in a 50:50 mix of sphagnum moss and perlite; potting soil will kill the plant. Place in a sunny spot and open windows regularly to allow insects in. Remove the flowers, which can weaken the plant. In winter, when dormant, move it away from heaters. Repot every year in late winter or early spring.

BUTTERWORT
Pinguicula—Mexican hybrids

TEMPERATURE 65–85°F (18–29°C)
LIGHT Bright indirect
HUMIDITY Moderate
CARE Easy
HEIGHT & SPREAD 6 x 4in (15 x 10cm)

The delicate small red, pink, or blue flowers that appear on this plant in summer belie its grisly secret. They are held on slim stems above a rosette of lime green or bronze foliage, which is covered with a sticky mucus that traps insects, such as fungus gnats. An enzyme in the leaves then digests the prey.

WATERING Keep moist by watering from above with unsoftened water. When the plant is dormant, usually in winter, reduce watering, allowing the top of the potting soil to dry out between waterings.

FEEDING No fertilizer is required, as most homes harbor a few insects; butterworts need just 2–3 insects per month to thrive.

PLANTING AND CARE Grow in a small 4–6in (10–15cm) pot in special carnivorous potting mixture or a 3:1:1 mix of silica sand, sphagnum moss, and perlite (never use potting soil). Set in bright light, out of direct summer sun. Plants can become dormant at any time of the year when they grow small fleshy leaves. Repot when dormant.

NORTH AMERICAN PITCHER PLANTS
Sarracenia species and hybrids

TEMPERATURE 23–77°F (-5–25°C)
LIGHT High
HUMIDITY Moderate
CARE Average
HEIGHT & SPREAD: Up to 12 x 6in (30 x 15cm)

These colorful carnivorous plants come in a range of sizes and produce pitchers in shades of burgundy, red, pink, and green, often with decorative vein patterns. The nectar around the pitcher mouth lures insects, which then fall in. While some *Sarracenia* will grow happily outside in too-wet soil, those from warmer climes make fascinating houseplants for a cool, bright room (they need cool winters). Pendulous red or green flowers appear in summer.

WATERING In summer, stand the plant pot in a tray of unsoftened water about ¼–½in (1–2cm) deep. In winter, remove the plant from the tray and keep the potting soil barely moist.

FEEDING Do not use a fertilizer on this plant; stand it outside or on a windowsill in summer, which will provide it with plenty of insect prey.

PLANTING AND CARE Plant in a small to medium-sized 4–6in (10–15cm) plastic pot in a special potting mixture usually available from a carnivorous plant supplier (or a 2:1:1 mix of fine fir bark, coarse lime-free hard sand, and perlite). Do not use potting soil, which will kill the plant. In late fall, it will become dormant and should be moved to a cool, bright room at 50°F (10°C) or colder until early spring. Repot every 2–3 years when dormant in fall, but do not plant in a large container, as it needs to be quite root-bound to thrive.

Sarracenia mitchelliana 'Bella' AGM

One of the many beautiful hybrids, 'Bella' has bright pink, red, and white vein patterns on the pitchers and lids, and bears bright red flowers in spring.

Sarracenia flava

Known as the yellow pitcher plant, this elegant type has tall, slender yellow–green pitchers with upright lids, and nodding yellow flowers in spring.

Sarracenia psittacina

Known as the parrot pitcher plant, this type will catch crawling insects with its rosette of decoratively veined red, white, or green horizontal traps. The dark spring flowers can vary in color.

Sarracenia purpurea

The purple pitcher plant has short fat pitchers in a deep burgundy color, with dark red or pink flowers in spring. It is quite hardy and can also be grown outside in the garden or on a patio.

Sarracenia 'Judith Hindle' AGM

The profusion of slim pitchers with frilly lids set this pretty hybrid apart. Young pitchers emerge green and mature to dark red, with marbled veining. Dark red flowers appear in spring.

FOLIAGE PLANTS

These leafy plants can be used as focal points or grouped together to create a calming green oasis. Choose a selection of plain-leaved types to create a simple backdrop for more intricately patterned foliage plants or add bright blooms to create a colorful display. Many foliage plants need only average care, with a few exceptions, and most are happy in rooms that receive little direct sunlight.

CHINESE EVERGREEN
Aglaonema commutatum

TEMPERATURE 60–77°F (16–25°C)
LIGHT Medium/Low
HUMIDITY Moderate
CARE Average
HEIGHT & SPREAD Up to 18 x 18in (45 x 45cm)
WARNING! All parts are toxic

This elegant plant has spear-shaped leaves with silver, cream, or pink patterning. All varieties aren't hard to care for, given warmth and sufficient moisture. Remove the small flowers to divert the plant's energy into growing leaves.

WATERING Keep the potting soil moist, but do not leave the pot in standing water, which may cause root rot. In winter, allow the top of the potting soil to dry out between waterings.

FEEDING Apply a quarter-strength balanced liquid fertilizer every other month from spring to fall.

PLANTING AND CARE Grow in a 6–8in (15–20cm) pot in aerated, well-draining potting soil mixed with a handful or two of perlite. Set in medium or low light, and keep away from drafts. Repot every 3 years in spring.

AMAZONIAN ELEPHANT'S EAR
Alocasia × amazonica AGM

TEMPERATURE 65–77°F (18–25°C)
LIGHT Bright indirect/Medium
HUMIDITY High
CARE Difficult
HEIGHT & SPREAD Up to 4 x 3ft
(1.2 x 1m)
WARNING! All parts are toxic

This show-stopper has large, dramatic foliage that sets it apart from the crowd. The arrow-shaped, dark green leaves are purple beneath and feature distinctive silver vein patterns and wavy edges. Remove the small flowers to allow the plant to focus its energy on the foliage.

WATERING Use unsoftened water to keep the potting soil moist from spring to fall; in winter, allow the top to dry out between waterings. Set on a tray of wet pebbles or install a room humidifier.

FEEDING Apply a half-strength fertilizer high in potassium and phosphorus and low in nitrogen every 2–3 weeks.

PLANTING AND CARE Grow in an equal mix of composted bark, aerated potting soil that includes peat moss, and sand in a 8–10in (25–30cm) pot. Set in a bright area, out of direct sun and drafts. Repot every 2–3 years.

ZEBRA PLANT
Aphelandra squarrosa

TEMPERATURE 55–77°F (13–25°C)
LIGHT Bright indirect
HUMIDITY Moderate to high
CARE Difficult
HEIGHT & SPREAD 24 x 24in
(60 x 60cm)

With dazzling striped green and cream foliage, this plant is ideal for a room with high humidity. The colorful fall flowers are composed of yellow bracts (modified petal-like leaves) around small orange blooms.

WATERING Using unsoftened water, keep the potting soil moist; dry soil may cause leaf drop. In winter, water when the top of the potting soil is almost dry. Set on a tray of wet pebbles or install a room humidifier.

FEEDING Apply a half-strength balanced liquid fertilizer once a week in spring and summer.

PLANTING AND CARE Plant in a 6–8in (15–20cm) pot in fast-draining, organic potting soil. Set in a bright spot, out of direct sun. Remove faded flower stems, and then prune to leave two sets of leaves at the bottom of the stems to keep plants compact. Repot annually in spring.

CAST IRON PLANT
Aspidistra elatior AGM

TEMPERATURE 45–85°F (8–29°C)
LIGHT Medium/Low
HUMIDITY Low
CARE Easy
HEIGHT & SPREAD 24 x 24in
(60 x 60cm)

Ideal for beginners, the cast iron plant is almost foolproof and can be tucked into low-light areas where few others will thrive. While the plain green type is not very exciting, plants with cream splashes, stripes, or spots inject more drama into a display.

WATERING Water when the top of the potting soil is dry; reduce watering in winter. Never allow the potting soil to become waterlogged or soggy.

FEEDING Apply a half-strength basic household fertilizer once a month when the plant is actively growing.

PLANTING AND CARE Plant in a 50:50 mix of aerated and multipurpose potting soils and a 5–8in (12.5–20cm) pot. Set in a medium-light area, well away from direct sun. Repot every 2–3 years in a container just one size larger than the original.

PAINTED LEAF BEGONIAS
Begonia species

TEMPERATURE 58–72°F (15–22°C)
LIGHT Bright indirect/Medium
HUMIDITY Moderate
CARE Average
HEIGHT & SPREAD Up to 36 x 18in (90 x 45cm)
WARNING! The roots are toxic

Forget the flowery bedding plants you see in summer; these demure beauties offer a completely different look. Celebrated for their decorative patterned foliage and small elegant flowers, there are hundreds of colors and forms to choose from. Most are derived from the *Begonia rex* species, which are also known as painted-leaf begonias because of their stunning leaf coloration. Taller cane types, such as the polka dot begonia, add structure to an indoor display, and have slightly larger flowers. The plants grow from tubers, but most are for sale as young plants.

WATERING Keep the potting soil moist, but not wet, from spring to fall; allow the top of the potting soil to dry out between waterings in winter. Stand on a tray of wet pebbles, but do not mist the leaves.

FEEDING Apply a half-strength feed every 2 weeks in spring and summer and monthly in fall and winter. Use a high-nitrogen fertilizer early in the season to encourage leaves, and a high-phosphorus fertilizer later in the season to encourage flowers.

PLANTING AND CARE Choose a pot that accommodates the plant's root ball easily. Plant in a 50:50 mix of aerated and multipurpose potting soils. Set in bright indirect or medium light and keep away from radiators and heaters in winter. Repot when root-bound in spring.

Begonia 'Rumba'

One of the many red-leaved *Rex* begonias, this elegant beauty has rich, pink-red foliage with near-black markings and red undersides. Stand it in bright indirect light for the best colors.

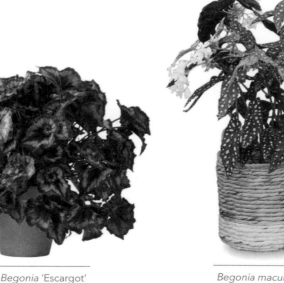

Begonia 'Escargot'

One of the *Rex* begonias, this popular variety has green and silver leaves that form a swirling pattern, like a snail's shell. The textured foliage is also covered with delicate pink hairs.

Begonia maculata

Known as the polka dot begonia, this large cane type is a real show-off, with its large green and white spotty leaves and cascading trusses of small cream flowers, which appear in summer. Its long stems will need staking.

Begonia soli-mutata

Few plants can beat this unusual begonia for leaf texture. While the dark burgundy and bright green markings on the heart-shaped foliage catch the eye, a closer inspection reveals the rough, sandpaperlike surface.

CROTON
Codiaeum variegatum

TEMPERATURE 60–76°F (15–25°C)
LIGHT Bright indirect
HUMIDITY High
CARE Average
HEIGHT & SPREAD Up to 5ft x 2ft 6in
(1.5 x 0.75m)
WARNING! All parts are toxic

The bright red, yellow, and green spear-shaped or lobed leaves of this potentially large shrub look best when set center stage against a neutral backdrop. Not the easiest plant to grow, it demands high humidity and constant warmth—find an area of your home or office with these ideal conditions.

WATERING Keep the potting soil moist with lukewarm water from spring to fall; allow the top to dry out between waterings in winter. Set it on a tray of wet pebbles, but do not mist the leaves.

FEEDING Apply a balanced liquid fertilizer every 2 weeks from spring to fall.

PLANTING AND CARE Plant in aerated potting soil in a pot that will accommodate the root ball. Repot every 2–3 years. Set in bright indirect light, away from drafts and heaters, and in constant warmth—never below 60°F (15°C). Wearing gloves, trim to keep it to size.

NEVER-NEVER PLANT
Ctenanthe burle-marxii

TEMPERATURE 50–76°F (10–25°C)
LIGHT Bright indirect
HUMIDITY Moderate
CARE Difficult
HEIGHT & SPREAD 24 x 18in
(60 x 45cm)

The never-never plant's profusion of striped dark and pale green leaves are given an extra lift with a splash of red on the undersides, lending a three-tone effect. This demanding, compact plant adds a glamorous note to a bright room.

WATERING Keep the potting soil moist from spring to fall, but allow the top of the potting soil to dry out between waterings in winter. If the leaves curl up, add more water. Stand on a tray of wet pebbles.

FEEDING Apply a half-strength balanced liquid fertilizer monthly from spring to fall.

PLANTING AND CARE Plant in a 5–6in (12.5–15cm) pot in an equal mix of aerated and multipurpose potting soils. Repot every 2–3 years when the plant becomes root-bound.

DUMB CANE
Dieffenbachia seguine

TEMPERATURE 61–73°F (16–23°C)
LIGHT Bright indirect/Medium
HUMIDITY Moderate
CARE Average
HEIGHT & SPREAD Up to
5 x 3ft (1.5 x 1m)
WARNING! All parts are toxic

The huge, patterned leaves of the dumb cane create an impressive feature in a large room or hallway in need of an eye-catching statement plant. The green, oval-shaped foliage features a splash or spots of cream in the center.

WATERING Keep the potting soil moist from spring to fall, and barely moist in winter. Stand on a tray of wet pebbles to increase the humidity.

FEEDING Apply a balanced liquid fertilizer every month from spring to fall.

PLANTING AND CARE Plant in aerated potting soil in a pot that fits the root ball. Stand in bright indirect or medium light. Wear gloves when pruning, as the sap is toxic. Repot every 2–3 years, or when the roots have filled the existing pot.

DRACAENA LEMON LIME
Dracaena deremensis

TEMPERATURE 60–75°F (15–24°C)
LIGHT Bright indirect/Medium
HUMIDITY Low to moderate
CARE Easy
HEIGHT & SPREAD Up to 4 x 3ft
(1.2 x 0.9m)
WARNING! All parts are toxic for pets

A great choice for beginners looking for a stalwart with foliage interest, the dracaena lemon lime produces fountains of strappy, variegated leaves, which form a rosette atop tall, canelike stems on mature plants. Choose from green leaves with a yellow central stripe, or foliage with green and yellow striped edges and a dark green center.

WATERING Keep the potting soil moist from spring to fall, and barely moist in the winter. Set on a tray of wet pebbles and keep at low to moderate humidity.

FEEDING Apply a half-strength balanced liquid fertilizer every 2 weeks from spring to fall.

PLANTING AND CARE Plant in aerated potting soil in a pot large enough to hold the root ball. Plants thrive best in bright indirect or medium light, but can survive (not grow) in low light. Air layer the stem, then remove the top of the plant once new growth has begun. Repot every 2–3 years.

MADAGASCAR DRAGON TREE
Dracaena marginata

TEMPERATURE 60–75°F (15–24°C)
LIGHT Bright indirect/Medium
HUMIDITY Low to moderate
CARE Easy
HEIGHT & SPREAD Up to 5 x 3ft
(1.5 x 0.9m)
WARNING! All parts are toxic for pets

The sprays of spiky leaves held on woody stems lend this popular plant an attractive, palmlike appearance. Tall and stately, with green, pink, and cream striped foliage, it is one of the best plants for removing toxins from the air. It is also very easy to grow.

WATERING Keep the potting soil moist from spring to fall, and barely moist in the winter.

FEEDING Apply a half-strength balanced liquid fertilizer every 2 weeks from spring to fall.

PLANTING AND CARE Plant in aerated potting soil in a pot that will fit the root ball. Prune the stems to limit the plant's size. Repot every 3 years or when root-bound.

JAPANESE ARALIA
Fatsia japonica

TEMPERATURE 60–76°F (10–25°C)
LIGHT Bright indirect/Medium
HUMIDITY Low to moderate
CARE Average
HEIGHT & SPREAD Up to 6 x 6ft
(2 x 2m)

The Japanese aralia is perfect for a room with medium light, since its large, glossy, hand-shaped leaves thrive in medium-light conditions. Choose from dark green or variegated leaves—the latter will need a little more light to retain their colors. Spherical cream flowers may appear in fall. This relatively undemanding plant is a great choice for beginners.

WATERING Keep the potting soil moist from spring to fall, and barely moist in the winter.

FEEDING Apply a half-strength balanced liquid fertilizer every 2 weeks from spring to late summer.

PLANTING AND CARE Plant in a pot large enough to accommodate the root ball with an equal mix of aerated and acidifying potting soils. Set in bright indirect or medium light; move the plant to a cool room in winter. Trim back to keep the plant in check. Repot every 2–3 years.

WEEPING FIG
Ficus benjamina

TEMPERATURE 65–75°F (16–24°C)
LIGHT Bright indirect/Medium
HUMIDITY Moderate
CARE Difficult
HEIGHT & SPREAD Up to 10 x 4ft
(3.5 x 1.2m)
WARNING! All parts are toxic

Tall and elegant, this plant should be given space to show off its arching stems of small green or variegated cream leaves. Not the easiest of plants, it has a tendency to drop its leaves, but it makes a striking focal point if you can provide the exact conditions it demands.

WATERING Use lukewarm unsoftened water and allow the top quarter of the potting soil to dry out between waterings. Keep a consistent schedule to avoid leaves turning yellow or black, or falling off.

FEEDING Apply a half-strength balanced liquid fertilizer once a month from spring to fall.

PLANTING AND CARE Plant in aerated potting soil in a pot that fits the root ball. Repot when the roots have filled the existing pot. In spring, replace the top layer of potting soil.

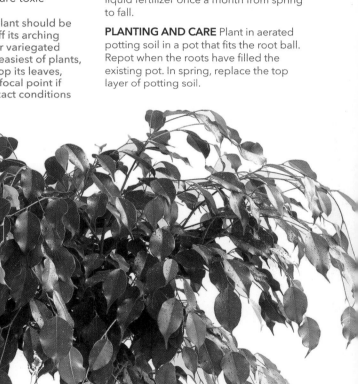

INDIA RUBBER PLANT
Ficus elastica

TEMPERATURE 60–75°F (15–24°C)
LIGHT Bright indirect/Medium
HUMIDITY Low to moderate
CARE Average
HEIGHT & SPREAD 6 x 4ft (1.8 x 1.2m)
WARNING! The sap is an irritant

Popular for its broad, glossy, dark green leaves and easygoing nature, the India rubber plant brings a treelike shape to a group of smaller plants. Rubber plants with variegated leaves will need more light, but all types are drought-tolerant.

WATERING Allow the top of the potting soil to dry out between waterings, and keep it barely moist in winter. Maintain low to moderate humidity for the plant.

FEEDING Apply a half-strength balanced liquid fertilizer once a month in spring and summer.

PLANTING AND CARE Plant in aerated potting soil with some perlite for added drainage in a pot large enough to accommodate the root ball. Set in bright indirect or medium light, away from drafts. Prune to keep the plant size in check. Repot every 2–3 years when root-bound.

FIDDLE-LEAF FIG
Ficus lyrata AGM

TEMPERATURE 60–75°F (15–24°C)
LIGHT Bright indirect
HUMIDITY Low to moderate
CARE Average
HEIGHT & SPREAD 6 x 4ft (1.8 x 1.2m)
WARNING! The sap is an irritant

The large, slightly lobed leaves of this tall, stately plant are shaped like a violin or fiddle, hence the name. They also have distinctive pale veins, and the stems sprout from a sturdy, treelike trunk. The plant is also available in the more compact 'Bambino' form.

WATERING Allow the top of the potting soil to dry out between waterings from spring to fall, and keep barely moist in winter. Ensure you do not overwater the plant, as the roots will rot in soggy conditions.

FEEDING Apply a half-strength balanced liquid fertilizer once a month in spring and summer.

PLANTING AND CARE Plant in a 3:1 mix of aerated potting soil and perlite in a pot that fits the root ball. Place in bright indirect light, away from direct sun and drafts. In winter, move it away from heaters. Repot every 2–3 years when root-bound.

NERVE PLANT
Fittonia albivensis Verschaffeltii Group AGM

TEMPERATURE 62–79°F (17–26°C)
LIGHT Bright indirect
HUMIDITY High
CARE Average
HEIGHT & SPREAD 6 x 8in (15 x 20cm)

The beautiful patterns on the foliage of the nerve plant make a striking feature. It is small enough for any room, but demands high humidity, so it is best kept in a humid room of your home or a terrarium. The dark or pale green leaves have bright pink veins and make a good match for the aluminum plant (*Pilea cadierei*), which is also small and requires similar conditions.

WATERING Keep the potting soil moist year-round, but avoid waterlogging—yellow leaves can indicate overwatering. Place on a tray of wet pebbles or install a room humidifier.

FEEDING Apply a quarter-strength balanced liquid fertilizer once a month from spring to fall.

PLANTING AND CARE Plant in aerated potting soil in a small 3–4in (7.5–10cm) pot. The nerve plant thrives in bright indirect light, away from direct sun. Remove the summer flowers to allow the plant to focus on its leaves. It needs warmth and moisture year-round, as well as high levels of humidity to keep its leaves healthy. Repot every 2–3 years when root-bound.

ETERNAL FLAME
Goeppertia crocata AGM
(syn. *Calathea crocata*)

TEMPERATURE 61–75°F (16–24°C)
LIGHT Bright indirect
HUMIDITY Moderate to high
CARE Difficult
HEIGHT & SPREAD 24 x 24in (60 x 60cm)

The torchlike orange summer flowers give this plant its name, but it can also be grown for its colorful foliage, which makes a feature in its own right. The broad, oval-shaped, slightly wrinkled leaves are green with a metallic sheen on the upper sides and dark burgundy beneath.

WATERING Keep the potting soil moist all year round, but guard against waterlogging. Maintain moderate to high humidity for the plant.

FEEDING From spring to early fall, apply a balanced liquid fertilizer monthly.

PLANTING AND CARE Plant in aerated potting soil in a medium-sized 5–6in (12.5–15cm) pot. Stand in a bright area out of direct sun, in a room with high humidity. Make sure that winter temperatures do not dip below 61°F (16°C). Repot every 2–3 years or when root-bound.

RATTLESNAKE PLANT
Goeppertia lancifolia
(syn. *Calathea lancifolia*) AGM

TEMPERATURE 60–75°F (15–24°C)
LIGHT Bright indirect/Medium
HUMIDITY Moderate
CARE Difficult
HEIGHT & SPREAD 30 x 18in (75 x 45cm)

This plant's star attraction is its dazzling, wavy-edge foliage, with its lime and dark green snakelike markings on the upper surfaces and burgundy shading beneath. A native of Brazil, it loves warm, humid conditions, so a kitchen would make an ideal home.

WATERING Keep the potting soil moist with unsoftened water from spring to fall; allow the top of the potting soil to dry out between waterings in winter. Place on a tray of wet pebbles or install a room humidifier.

FEEDING Apply a half-strength balanced liquid fertilizer every 2 weeks from spring to fall.

PLANTING AND CARE Use a 2:1 mix of aerated potting soil and perlite and plant in a 5–6in (12.5–15cm) pot. Stand in bright or medium light, out of direct sun and drafts. Keep warm all year round. Repot every 2–3 years when root-bound.

PEACOCK PLANT
Goeppertia makoyana
(syn. *Cathea makoyana*) AGM

TEMPERATURE 61–75°F (16–24°C)
LIGHT Bright indirect
HUMIDITY High
CARE Difficult
HEIGHT & SPREAD 24 x 24in
(60 x 60cm)

The silver leaves of this crowd-pleaser are impossible to overlook, with darker green brush strokes on the upper surface and burgundy markings beneath. While not the easiest to care for, the plant's striking appearance makes it well worth the effort.

WATERING Use unsoftened water to keep the potting soil moist from spring to fall, and barely moist in the winter. To increase humidity, place on a tray of wet pebbles or install a room humidifier.

FEEDING Apply a half-strength balanced liquid fertilizer every 2 weeks from spring to fall.

PLANTING AND CARE Plant in a 2:1 mix of aerated potting soil and perlite in a 6–8in (15–20cm) pot. Set in bright light, out of direct sun and drafts. Keep warm all year round. Repot every 2–3 years when root-bound.

VELVET PLANT
Gynura aurantiaca

TEMPERATURE 60–75°F (15–24°C)
LIGHT Bright indirect
HUMIDITY Moderate
CARE Average
HEIGHT & SPREAD 8 x 8in (20 x 20cm)

The soft, velvety leaves of this compact plant are simply irresistible and call out to be touched. Fine purple hairs cover the lobed, metallic-green foliage, giving it a downy, two-tone appearance, while the leafy stems trail elegantly over the sides of a pot.

WATERING Keep the potting soil moist from spring to fall, and only barely moist in winter. Avoid wetting the foliage, which should be kept dry. Set on a tray of wet pebbles, but do not mist, as this causes spots on the leaves.

FEEDING Apply a half-strength balanced liquid fertilizer every 2 weeks from spring to fall.

PLANTING AND CARE Plant in an equal mix of multipurpose and aerated potting soils in a wide 5–6in (12.5–15cm) pot. Set in bright light, out of direct sun. Pinch back the stem tips to create a bushier plant, as well as the yellow flowers, which have a rather unpleasant smell. Repot every 2–3 years or when root-bound.

POLKA DOT PLANT
Hypoestes phyllostachya AGM

TEMPERATURE 65–80°F (18–27°C)
LIGHT Bright indirect
HUMIDITY Moderate
CARE Average
HEIGHT & SPREAD 10 x 10in
(25 x 25cm)

Compact and colorful, this plant's green, heart-shaped leaves are speckled with pink, red, or cream spots, although on many varieties they look more like splashes than the round polka dots suggested by the name. Try a few varieties in different colors in a terrarium or bottle garden. Small magenta flowers appear in summer.

WATERING Allow the top of the potting soil to dry out between waterings from spring to fall, and keep barely moist in winter. Stand on a tray of wet pebbles to increase humidity.

FEEDING Apply a half-strength balanced liquid fertilizer once a month in spring and summer, then every other month in fall and winter as long as it has new leaves.

PLANTING AND CARE Plant in aerated, well-draining, and loose potting soil in a 4–5in (10–12.5cm) pot. Stand in bright indirect light, ideally in a room of your home with high humidity. Pinch back the stem tips to create a bushier plant. Repot every 2–3 years or when the plant becomes root-bound.

ALUMINUM PLANT
Pilea cadierei AGM

TEMPERATURE 60–75°F (15–24°C)
LIGHT Medium
HUMIDITY Moderate
CARE Average
HEIGHT & SPREAD 12 x 10in
(30 x 25cm)
WARNING! All parts are toxic

The lacy, silver markings on the foliage of this pretty little plant give it its name, while an easygoing nature makes it a good choice for beginners. Use it to add sparkle to a leafy collection in a lightly shaded room.

WATERING Keep the potting soil moist from spring to fall; allow the top of the potting soil to dry out between waterings in winter.

FEEDING Apply a half-strength balanced liquid fertilizer every 2 weeks from spring to fall.

PLANTING AND CARE Use a 2:1 mix of aerated potting soil and perlite and plant in a 5–6in (12.5–15cm) pot. Stand in medium light, out of direct sun, and keep the plant warm year-round. Pinch back the flower buds on the stem tips to keep the plant bushy. Repot every year or two when root-bound.

MISSIONARY PLANT
Pilea peperomioides AGM

TEMPERATURE 60–75°F (15–24°C)
LIGHT Bright indirect/Medium
HUMIDITY Moderate
CARE Average
HEIGHT & SPREAD 12 x 12in
(30 x 30cm)
WARNING! All parts are toxic

Balanced on the stems like spinning plates, the round leaves of this unusual plant create an intriguing display, elevating it to the top of many plant collectors' wish lists. The loose dome of leaves looks great on a windowsill or table in an area with medium light.

WATERING Allow the top of the potting soil to dry out between waterings from spring to fall; keep it barely moist in winter.

FEEDING Apply a half-strength balanced liquid fertilizer every 2 weeks from spring to fall.

PLANTING AND CARE Plant in a 2:1 mix of aerated potting soil and perlite in a 5–6in (12.5–15cm) pot. Stand in medium light, out of direct sun and away from drafts. Keep the plant warm year-round, and repot every 1–2 years in spring when it is root-bound.

BRAZILIAN COLEUS
Plectranthus oertendahlii AGM

TEMPERATURE 60–75°F (15–24°C)
LIGHT Medium/Low
HUMIDITY Low
CARE Easy
HEIGHT & SPREAD 8 x 24in
(20 x 60cm)

Grown for its handsome, rough, silver-veined foliage and spires of small white spring flowers, the lax stems of this easy-care plant make it a good choice for a tall pot. It thrives in medium light, but will also grow happily in gloomier conditions, adding color and texture to rooms without any direct sun.

WATERING Allow the top of the potting soil to dry out between waterings from spring to fall. In winter, allow the soil to dry out even more.

FEEDING Apply a fish emulsion or half-strength balanced liquid fertilizer once a month from spring to fall.

PLANTING AND CARE Use a 2:1 mix of aerated potting soil and perlite and plant in a 5–6in (12.5–15cm) pot. Set in medium light, out of direct sun. Repot every 2–3 years when root-bound.

CHINA DOLL PLANT
Radermachera sinica AGM

TEMPERATURE 54–75°F (12–24°C)
LIGHT Bright indirect
HUMIDITY Low to moderate
CARE Average
HEIGHT & SPREAD Up to 4 x 6ft
(1.8 x 1.2m)

This handsome plant will fill an empty corner in a bright room with its elegant leafy stems. The glossy foliage is a rich green in color and is divided up into small leaflets, which lend this treelike plant a light, airy look.

WATERING From spring to early fall, water when the top of the potting soil feels dry. Reduce watering in winter so the potting soil is barely moist.

FEEDING Apply a half-strength balanced liquid fertilizer every 2 weeks from spring to fall.

PLANTING AND CARE Plant in aerated potting soil in a pot that will accommodate the root ball. Stand in bright light, out of direct sun. Pinch back stem tips in spring to keep the plant bushy and full. Repot this fast-growing plant every 2 years.

AFRICAN SPEAR
Sansevieria cylindrica

TEMPERATURE 60–75°F (15–24°C)
LIGHT Bright indirect/Medium
HUMIDITY Low
CARE Easy
HEIGHT & SPREAD 30 x 12in
(75 x 30cm)
WARNING! All parts are toxic

Like its cousin the snake plant, the African spear will help to purify the air, and it is easy to care for. Its tall, slim, cylindrical leaves look like javelins, and the gray-green banding on the leaves adds to the decorative effect. Position the plant where the brittle foliage will not get broken off.

WATERING Allow the top of the potting soil to dry out between waterings from spring to fall; water once a month in winter.

FEEDING Apply a half-strength cactus fertilizer once a month from spring to fall. Don't use a fertilizer with nitrates.

PLANTING AND CARE Use a cactus potting soil and plant in a pot that will only just fit the roots; it likes to be cramped. Set out of direct sun; it tolerates some low light, but the spears may stretch to the light. Repot only when tightly root-bound.

VARIEGATED SNAKE PLANT
Sansevieria trifasciata var. *laurentii* AGM

TEMPERATURE 60–75°F (15–24°C)
LIGHT Medium
HUMIDITY Low
CARE Easy
HEIGHT & SPREAD 30 x 12in
(75 x 30cm)
WARNING! All parts are toxic

One of the best plants for purifying the air, the snake plant—or mother-in-law's tongue, as it is also known—produces a tight cluster of green and silver swordlike foliage with a yellow trim. Thriving on neglect (overwatering will rot it), this plant is almost bullet-proof.

WATERING Allow the top of the potting soil to dry out between waterings from spring to fall; water once a month in winter.

FEEDING Apply a half-strength cactus fertilizer once a month from spring to fall. Don't use a fertilizer with nitrates.

PLANTING AND CARE Use a cactus potting soil and plant in a pot that will just accommodate the roots—it likes a snug fit. Set in medium light, out of direct sun. Repot only when tightly root-bound.

HAWAIIAN SCHEFFLERA TREE
Schefflera arboricola AGM

TEMPERATURE 60–75°F (15–24°C)
LIGHT Bright indirect
HUMIDITY Low to moderate
CARE Average
HEIGHT & SPREAD 8 x 4ft
(2.4 x 1.2m)
WARNING! All parts are toxic

This impressive plant is loved for its hand-shaped green or variegated leaves. It is efficient at filtering indoor air pollution, making it a perfect plant for your home or office.

WATERING Allow the top of the potting soil to dry out between waterings from spring to fall; water once a month in winter.

FEEDING Apply a half-strength balanced liquid fertilizer every month in spring and summer.

PLANTING AND CARE Plant in a heavy pot that will fit the root ball, in a 2:1 mix of aerated potting soil and sand. Keep out of direct sun in a warm room. Prune in spring, and repot every 2 years.

COLEUS
Solenostemon scutellarioides hybrids

TEMPERATURE 60–75°F (15–24°C)
LIGHT Bright indirect
HUMIDITY Moderate
CARE Average
HEIGHT & SPREAD 24 x 12in
(60 x 30cm)
WARNING! All parts toxic to pets

With a huge choice of leaf shapes and colors—from lime green and lipstick pink to brooding burgundy, burnt orange, and everything in between—there is a coleus to suit any design scheme. The fancy foliage makes a great partner for plain-leaved plants, or use some of the muted colors as foils for flowers.

WATERING Keep the potting soil moist from spring to fall; allow the top of the potting soil to dry out between waterings in winter.

FEEDING Apply a fish emulsion or half-strength balanced liquid fertilizer once a month from spring to fall.

PLANTING AND CARE Grow in an equal mix of multipurpose and aerated potting soils in a 6in (15cm) pot. Pinch back stem tips in spring to keep the plant bushy and full. Set in bright light, but out of direct sun. Prune the stems back by two-thirds in late winter or early spring (see pp.194–95).

STROMANTHE
Stromanthe sanguinea 'Triostar'

TEMPERATURE 60–75°F (15–24°C)
LIGHT Bright indirect
HUMIDITY High
CARE Difficult
HEIGHT & SPREAD 18 x 24in
(45 x 60cm)

A jewel among foliage plants, few can compete with the stromanthe's striking leaves, splashed with shades of pink, red, green, and cream. It needs space to show off its spreading, spear-shaped foliage, and is best displayed in a plain container that complements but does not compete with its dazzling hues.

WATERING Keep the potting soil moist from spring to summer, and water less frequently in winter. Set on a tray of wet pebbles or install a room humidifier.

FEEDING Apply a half-strength balanced liquid fertilizer every 2 weeks from spring to late fall.

PLANTING AND CARE Plant in an equal mix of multipurpose and aerated potting soils in a 5–6in (12.5–15cm) pot—shallow containers are ideal. Stand the plant in a bright spot, out of direct sun and drafts, in your home or office. Repot every 2–3 years.

ARROWHEAD PLANT
Syngonium podophyllum AGM

TEMPERATURE 60–85°F (15–29°C)
LIGHT Bright indirect/Medium
HUMIDITY Moderate
CARE Easy
HEIGHT & SPREAD Up to 3 x 2ft
(90 x 60cm)
WARNING! All parts are toxic

The arrow-shaped cream and green variegated foliage of the arrowhead plant will add a jungly note to a foliage display in a bright or medium-light room. It is usually sold as a compact foliage plant, but, if left to its own devices, it will become a lovely hanging plant.

WATERING Allow the top of the potting soil to dry out between waterings from spring to late fall; reduce watering slightly in winter. To increase humidity, set on a tray of wet pebbles.

FEEDING Apply a half-strength balanced liquid fertilizer every 2 weeks from spring to fall.

PLANTING AND CARE Plant in aerated potting soil in a 6–8in (15–20cm) pot. It will thrive in a bright spot out of direct sun, ideally in a humid area of your home or office. Prune every year in spring to keep it compact and bushy, and when it reaches an ideal size, do not repot, but replace the top layer of the potting soil annually in spring.

MOSES IN THE CRADLE
Tradescantia spathacea

TEMPERATURE 60–80°F (15–27°C)
LIGHT Bright indirect
HUMIDITY Moderate
CARE Easy
HEIGHT & SPREAD 24 x 24in
(60 x 60cm)

This plant's green and purple sword-shaped leaves make an eye-catching bouquet. Small, white flowers appear throughout the year, nestled between the leaves, but the star attraction is the foliage. This compact plant will thrive in any room of your home with moderate humidity.

WATERING Allow the top of the potting soil to dry out between waterings from spring to fall; keep it barely moist in winter. To increase humidity, set on a tray of wet pebbles.

FEEDING Apply a half-strength balanced liquid fertilizer once a month in spring and summer.

PLANTING AND CARE Plant in a 2:1 mix of aerated potting soil and sand or perlite in a 6–8in (15–20cm) pot. Set in a bright spot, out of direct sun; it tolerates some lower light, but may lose its purple tones. Repot every 2–3 years.

ZZ PLANT
Zamioculcas zamiifolia

TEMPERATURE 60–75°F (15–24°C)
LIGHT Bright indirect/Medium
HUMIDITY Low
CARE Easy
HEIGHT & SPREAD 30 x 24in
(75 x 60cm)
WARNING! All parts are toxic

The long, leafy stems of the ZZ plant form a large, vase-shaped plant that will grow almost anywhere, as it tolerates both sun and shade, as well as low levels of humidity. Perfect for beginners, the glossy foliage makes a good foil for more glamorous leaves and flowers.

WATERING Allow the top of the potting soil to dry out between waterings from spring to fall; water once a month in winter.

FEEDING Apply a half-strength balanced liquid fertilizer every other month while actively growing.

PLANTING AND CARE Grow in a 2:1 mix of aerated potting soil and sand in a pot that fits the root ball. Medium or bright indirect light is ideal, but it will also grow in gloomier spots. Trim in spring to create a good shape. Repot every 2–3 years.

SPINELESS YUCCA
Yucca elephantipes AGM

TEMPERATURE 50–80°F (10–27°C)
LIGHT High/Bright indirect
HUMIDITY Low
CARE Easy
HEIGHT & SPREAD 5 x 2ft 6in
(1.5 x 0.75m)
WARNING! All parts toxic to pets

This yucca's spiky, swordlike foliage grows from a palmlike trunk, forming a dramatic sculptural shape that makes a bold statement in any room.

WATERING Allow the top of the potting soil to dry out between waterings from spring to fall; water once a month in winter.

FEEDING Apply a half-strength balanced liquid fertilizer monthly in spring and summer.

PLANTING AND CARE Plant in a 2:1 mix of aerated soil and sand in a pot that fits the root ball. If the plant gets top heavy, cut the trunk halfway down. New growth will develop below the cut. Repot every 2–3 years. Keep the plant out of intense afternoon sun in summer, as the leaves may become scorched.

CACTI

From the spiky and wonderfully weird, to elegant trailers with smooth stems, cacti are technically succulents, but are usually considered to belong in their own distinct category. Many are perfect for a sunny windowsill display or simple hanging basket, and their ability to store water in their leaves and stems, allowing them to survive extended periods of drought, makes them ideal for beginners. Not all are desert dwellers, and a few, including the Christmas cactus (see p.165), live naturally on trees in tropical forests and require shadier conditions and humidity.

OLD MAN CACTUS
Cephalocereus senilis

TEMPERATURE 50-90°F (10-32°C)
LIGHT High/Bright indirect in summer
HUMIDITY Low
CARE Easy
HEIGHT & SPREAD 12 x 4in (30 x 10cm)

Covered in fine white hairs that resemble an old man's beard, this cactus's weird appearance is guaranteed to create a talking point. The tall, unbranched columnar stems grow in clusters, and the silvery hairs are most prevalent on young plants. The cactus's red, yellow, or white flowers rarely appear.

WATERING Allow the top ½–¾in (1–2cm) of potting soil to dry out completely between waterings. In winter, reduce watering to once or twice during the season.

FEEDING Apply a fertilizer for cacti once a month in spring and summer.

PLANTING AND CARE Wearing protective gloves, plant in a small 4in (10cm) pot in cactus soil (or in an equal mix of aerated potting soil, sand, and perlite). Set in sun, but move to a cool but bright room (unheated, if possible) in winter. Repot young plants annually in spring, and mature cacti every 2 years.

PERUVIAN APPLE CACTUS
Cereus forbesii

TEMPERATURE 50–90°F (10–32°C)
LIGHT High/Bright indirect in summer
HUMIDITY Low
CARE Easy
HEIGHT & SPREAD Up to 36 x 6in (90 x 15cm)

This plant's classic cactus shape and form makes it a great addition to a collection, creating height and structure at the back of a display. The gray-green stems are covered with brown spines, and in summer they bear large, scented white or pink flowers up to 6in (15cm) in diameter, which open at night and close at dawn.

WATERING Water when the top ½in (1cm) of potting soil is dry. Water once or twice in winter when the plant is dormant.

FEEDING Apply a cactus fertilizer once a month in summer.

PLANTING AND CARE Wearing protective gloves, plant in a heavy 6–8in (15–20cm) pot to prevent the plant toppling over, in cactus soil (or an equal mix of aerated sand, potting soil, and perlite). Set in the sun, but move to a cool, bright room in winter. Repot young plants annually, and then every 2 years.

ORCHID CACTUS
Disocactus flagelliformis AGM

TEMPERATURE 40–75°F (4–24°C)
LIGHT Bright indirect
HUMIDITY Moderate
CARE Average
HEIGHT & SPREAD 24 x 24in (60 x 60cm)

With its flat, thin, scallop-edged stems, this tropical cactus is ideal for a hanging basket in a bright room. In spring, the plant's large, red, funnel-shaped flowers are the real stars of the show.

WATERING Water regularly from spring to early fall, allowing the soil to dry out before watering to avoid root rot. Keep plants barely moist in winter. Mist occasionally with unsoftened water during hot summers.

FEEDING Apply a half-strength, high-potassium fertilizer once every 2 weeks from spring to summer.

PLANTING AND CARE Plant in a 4in (10cm) pot or basket in epiphytic cactus potting soil (or a 4:1 mix of aerated potting soil and sharp sand). Ideally, keep this cactus in bright indirect light and between 60–75°F (16–24°C) in the day and 40–55°F (4–12°C) at night from spring to fall. In winter, move to a cool, low-light room, then return to bright indirect light in spring. Plants flower best when root-bound, so do not repot.

ZIGZAG CACTUS
Epiphyllum anguliger

TEMPERATURE 52–77°F (11–25°C)
LIGHT Bright indirect/Medium
HUMIDITY Moderate
CARE Average
HEIGHT & SPREAD 24 x 24in (60 x 60cm)

The mound of leaves, with a wavy style resembling a zigzag pattern, have pushed this unusual plant to the top of many a cactus-lover's wish list. The fragrant, pale yellow flowers add to its charms in fall.

WATERING Water regularly from spring to early fall, allowing the soil to dry out between waterings. Reduce watering by half in winter, then resume normal watering in spring.

FEEDING In summer, when the flower buds form, apply a high-potassium fertilizer every 2 weeks until the blooms open.

PLANTING AND CARE Plant this cactus in a 4–6in (10–15cm) pot or basket in epiphytic cactus potting soil (or a 4:1 mix of aerated potting soil and sharp sand). Keep the plant at 61–77°F (16–25°C) from spring to fall. In winter, move to a cool, shady place at 52–57°F (11–14°C); this will encourage flowering. Repot young plants annually in spring; just replenish the potting soil of mature plants.

DEVIL'S TONGUE
Ferocactus latispinus AGM

TEMPERATURE 50–86°F (10–30°C)
LIGHT High/Bright indirect in summer
HUMIDITY Low
CARE Easy
HEIGHT & SPREAD Up to 10 x 10in
(25 x 25cm)

This spiky barrel-shaped cactus has great stage presence. The plump, round stem is covered with thick, red, hooked spines (which give the plant its name) and needlelike cream spines that combine to form a ball of colorful spikes. Purple or yellow flowers appear in late summer on mature plants.

WATERING Allow the top ¾in (2cm) of potting soil to dry out between waterings from spring to fall. Water just once or twice in winter.

FEEDING Apply a cactus fertilizer every 3–4 weeks from spring to late summer.

PLANTING AND CARE Wearing protective gloves, plant in a pot large enough to stabilize the cactus. Plant in cactus potting soil (or a 3:1:1 mix of aerated potting soil, sand, and perlite). Set on a sunny windowsill, moving the plant away from the window a little in midsummer. In winter, move to a cool, bright, unheated room. Repot young plants annually, and mature plants every 2 years.

PINCUSHION CACTUS
Mammillaria species

TEMPERATURE 45–86°F (7–30°C)
LIGHT High/Bright indirect in summer
HUMIDITY Low
CARE Easy
HEIGHT & SPREAD Up to 6 x 8in
(15 x 30cm) for most species

These diminutive cacti are popular houseplants, with most fitting neatly on a sunny windowsill and flowering regularly in summer. They are round or form short columns, and have tiny spines along ridges or on top of the little bumps that cover the surface of most of these cacti. Pink, purple, orange, or cream flowers form a ring at the top of the plant in summer.

WATERING Allow the top ¾in (2cm) of potting soil to dry out between waterings from spring to fall. Water just once or twice in winter when the plant is dormant.

FEEDING Apply a cactus fertilizer every 3–4 weeks from midspring to late summer.

PLANTING AND CARE Wearing protective gloves, plant in a small 3–4in (7.5–10cm) pot in cactus potting soil (or a 3:1:1 mix of aerated potting soil, sand, and perlite). Set on a sunny windowsill, but move the cactus away from the window in midsummer. In winter, set in a cool, bright, unheated room with low humidity. Repot young plants annually, and mature plants every 2 years.

Mammillaria polythele f. *nuda*

Small and columnar, this little cactus has the typical knobby appearance of most pincushion cacti. Its pink flowers appear over a long period from spring to summer.

Mammillaria saboae subsp. *haudeana*

This unusual variety produces small, round stems from a larger central ribbed stem. The pink flowers appear in summer like shooting stars.

BUNNY EARS CACTUS
Opuntia microdasys AGM

TEMPERATURE 50–86°F
(10–30°C)
LIGHT High/Bright indirect in summer
HUMIDITY Low
CARE Easy
HEIGHT & SPREAD 12 x 18in
(30 x 45cm)

This pretty cactus produces oval-shaped, flattened green stems dotted with clusters of tiny bristlelike spines ("glochids") that grow in pairs to resemble rabbits' ears. In summer, yellow bowl-shaped flowers appear.

WATERING Water weekly from spring to early fall, allowing the potting soil to dry out between waterings. Water once or twice in winter when dormant.

FEEDING Apply a cactus fertilizer every 6–8 weeks from spring to early fall.

PLANTING AND CARE Wearing gloves, plant in a pot that will not restrict the cactus's roots, and use a cactus potting soil (or a 3:1:1 mix of aerated potting soil, sand, and perlite). Place in a bright spot away from direct sun in summer, and in a cool room in winter. Repot young plants annually, and mature plants every 2 years.

GOLDEN BALL CACTUS
Parodia leninghausii AGM

TEMPERATURE 50–86°F
(10–30°C)
LIGHT High/Bright indirect in summer
HUMIDITY Low
CARE Easy
HEIGHT & SPREAD Up to
18 x 6in (45 x 15cm)

This plant creates a mini desert scene with its clusters of compact prickly stems. Its common name can be confusing because mature plants have a columnar rather than ball shape, and it may also be labeled as *Notocactus* rather than *Parodia*. Bright yellow flowers appear on a woolly crown in summer on mature plants.

WATERING Water from spring to fall only when the top ¾in (2cm) of potting soil has dried out. Water just once or twice in winter when the plant is dormant.

FEEDING Apply a cactus fertilizer every 6–8 weeks from spring to late summer.

PLANTING AND CARE Wearing protective gloves, plant in a 3–6in (7.5–15cm) pot, depending on the size of the cactus. Add a layer of hard sand to the pot and top up with cactus potting soil (or a 3:1:1 mix of aerated potting soil, sand, and perlite). Place in sun, but keep out of direct sun in summer. Move to a bright but cool room in winter. Repot young plants annually, and then every 2 years.

CHRISTMAS CACTUS
Schlumbergera × bridgesii

TEMPERATURE 54–80°F (12–27°C)
LIGHT Bright indirect
HUMIDITY Moderate
CARE Average
HEIGHT & SPREAD 18 x 18in
(45 x 45cm)

Prized for its bright pink flowers, which open up at Christmastime, this tropical cactus also produces flat, segmented trailing stems all year round.

WATERING Keep the potting soil moist, but not wet. Reduce watering for a few weeks after flowering in late winter when the plant rests, and again from midfall until buds develop in early winter. Place on a tray of wet pebbles.

FEEDING Apply a half-strength liquid indoor fertilizer every 2 weeks in spring and summer. Never feed after October 1.

PLANTING AND CARE Plant in a small pot in cactus potting soil (or a 3:1:1 mix of aerated potting soil, leafmold, and hard sand). After flowering, move to a cool room, then increase the temperature, and water and fertilize it during the growing seasons. Repot in early spring.

SUCCULENTS

These drought-lovers are grown mainly for their striking foliage, which comes in all shapes and sizes, from tall and spiky to small, round, and velvety. The flowers, if they appear, are often a surprise, their bright colors providing a vivid contrast to the fleshy leaves. Succulents are easy to grow, and because their foliage acts as the perfect water-storage unit, they can suffer long periods of neglect. Just give them a sunny position and water them very occasionally to keep them happy.

PINWHEEL
Aeonium haworthii

TEMPERATURE 50–75°F (10–24°C)
LIGHT High/Bright indirect
HUMIDITY Low
CARE Easy
HEIGHT & SPREAD Up to 24 x 18in (60 x 45cm)

This sculptural succulent adds height and character to a mixed display on a windowsill. The branched stems are topped with rosettes of gray-green fleshy leaves, and in late spring, small pale yellow or pink-tinged flowers rise up above the foliage. Look out for variegated types, too, which feature yellow and pink-edged leaves.

WATERING Water from fall to spring, when the top of the potting soil feels dry; keep the soil almost dry in summer, when the plant may go dormant in hot periods.

FEEDING Apply a half-strength balanced liquid fertilizer once a month from winter to late spring.

PLANTING AND CARE Plant in a 6in (15cm) pot in cactus potting soil. Display in bright light, out of direct sun in summer. After flowering, the leafy rosette will die, but plants will grow. Repot every 2–3 years in spring.

BLACK ROSE AEONIUM
Aeonium 'Zwartkop' AGM

TEMPERATURE 50–75°F (10–24°C)
LIGHT High/Bright indirect
HUMIDITY Low
CARE Easy
HEIGHT & SPREAD Up to 2 x 2ft
(60 x 60cm)

One of the most sought-after aeoniums, this statuesque variety features rosettes of dark purple, almost black, leaves on tall, branching stems. In early spring, mature plants bear small, starry, yellow flowers. Grow it as a houseplant all year round, or on a patio outside in summer.

WATERING Water from fall to spring, when the top of the potting soil feels dry; keep the soil almost dry in summer, when it may go dormant in hot weather.

FEEDING Apply a half-strength balanced liquid fertilizer once a month from winter to late spring.

PLANTING AND CARE Grow in cactus potting soil in a 6in (15cm) pot. Set in bright light, out of direct summer sun. The leafy rosette will die after flowering, but new plants will grow to replace the old one. Repot every 2–3 years in spring.

CENTURY PLANT
Agave americana AGM

TEMPERATURE 50–86°F (10–30°C)
LIGHT High/Bright indirect
HUMIDITY Low
CARE Easy
HEIGHT & SPREAD Up to 3 x 3ft
(90 x 90cm)
WARNING! The sap is toxic

In arid areas, this spiky plant grows into a huge, impressive plant, gracing parks and landscapes with its spiny blue leaves, each sporting a white stripe down the center. Grown indoors in a pot, it will remain more compact, but can still form a large plant, so give its spreading leaves space to shine.

WATERING Water from fall to spring, when the top of the potting soil feels dry; keep almost dry through winter.

FEEDING Apply a half-strength balanced liquid fertilizer every 2 weeks from early spring to early fall.

PLANTING AND CARE Plant in cactus potting soil in a pot that will just fit the root ball. Stand in high or bright indirect light. Repot every 1–2 years, wearing gloves to protect your hands. Keep it compact by replenishing the potting soil, trimming the roots, and repotting it in a pot that's either the same size or one size larger.

QUEEN VICTORIA AGAVE
Agave victoria-reginae

TEMPERATURE 50–85°F (10–29°C)
LIGHT High/Bright indirect
HUMIDITY Low
CARE Easy
HEIGHT & SPREAD Up to 2 x 2ft
(60 x 60cm)
WARNING! The sap is toxic

The thick, triangular leaves of this agave have white edges and black tips, which you only notice on close inspection, so display where these details can be admired. An easy-care succulent, its textural dome of leaves makes a great partner for echeverias, aeoniums, and houseleeks (*Sempervivum*).

WATERING Water from fall to spring, when the top of the potting soil feels dry; in winter, allow the potting soil to dry out, watering just once or twice.

FEEDING Apply a half-strength balanced liquid fertilizer 2–3 times during the growing period from spring to fall.

PLANTING AND CARE Plant in cactus potting soil in a pot that just fits the root ball. Stand in high or bright indirect light. Repot every 2–3 years or when root-bound.

JADE PLANT
Crassula ovata AGM

TEMPERATURE 60–77°F (15–25°C)
LIGHT High/Bright indirect
HUMIDITY Low
CARE Easy
HEIGHT & SPREAD 3 x 3ft (90 x 90cm)
WARNING! The sap is toxic

Sometimes known as the money tree, due its association with wealth and prosperity in some Asian cultures, this plant is also renowned for being almost indestructible, soldiering on through extended periods of neglect. Mature plants look like beautiful bonsai trees, with their thick, branched stems and oval-shaped, fleshy, red-edged leaves.

WATERING From spring to fall, allow the top of the potting soil to dry out between waterings. In winter, water just enough to prevent the leaves shriveling.

FEEDING Apply a half-strength balanced liquid fertilizer 2–3 times during the growing period from spring to fall.

PLANTING AND CARE Wearing gloves, plant in a 4–6in (10–15cm) pot in a 3:1 mix of aerated potting soil and sharp sand. Repot only when root-bound.

ALOE VERA
Aloe vera AGM

TEMPERATURE 50–80°F (10–27°C)
LIGHT High/Bright indirect
HUMIDITY Low
CARE Easy
HEIGHT & SPREAD 2 x 2ft (60 x 60cm)

Some people grow this architectural aloe for its handsome, spiky green leaves, but its benefits go far beyond aesthetic appeal. One of the best plants for purifying the air, the sap from aloe leaves can also be used to soothe burns, including sunburn.

WATERING From spring to fall, allow the top of the potting soil to dry out between waterings. In winter, keep the potting soil almost dry.

FEEDING Apply a half-strength balanced liquid fertilizer 2–3 times during the growing period from spring to fall.

PLANTING AND CARE Plant in cactus potting soil in a pot that just fits the root ball. Stand in bright indirect light in summer. Repot every 2–3 years in spring, and pot baby offsets that appear next to the mother plant in 3–4in (7.5–10cm) pots.

ECHEVERIA
Echeveria species

TEMPERATURE 50–86°F (10–30°C)
LIGHT High/Bright indirect
HUMIDITY Low
CARE Easy
HEIGHT & SPREAD Up to 4 x 12in
(10 x 30cm)

These beautiful little succulents form tight rosettes of spoon-shaped, blue-green, red, purple, or variegated leaves. Line up a few with different colors and forms (there are hundreds to choose from) on a sunny windowsill, or include them as part of a group of contrasting succulents. If grown in sufficient light, mature plants produce tall pink or yellow stems that rise up from the center of the rosette, topped with lantern-shaped flowers.

WATERING From spring to fall, allow the top of the potting soil to dry out between waterings; do not water in winter when dormant.

FEEDING Apply a half-strength balanced liquid fertilizer 2–3 times during the growing period from spring to fall.

PLANTING AND CARE Grow echeverias in a 4–6in (10–15cm) pot in a 3:1 mix of aerated potting soil and sharp sand. Stand in bright light, out of direct sun in summer, and in a cool, sunny area in winter when dormant. Repot every 2–3 years in spring or when root-bound. Baby plantlets appear next to the mother plant and can be left in place to increase the size of the original plant, or planted separately in a 4in (10cm) pot of their own.

Echeveria agavoides 'Taurus'

Also sold as 'Red Taurus', this beautiful form produces a dark, burgundy-red leaf rosette, and in summer, red and yellow flowers appear on tall stems.

Echeveria elegans AGM

One of the most popular echeverias, this elegant species has blue-green leaves with burgundy edges, and in summer it produces long pink stems topped with pink and yellow flowers.

Echeveria secunda var. *glauca*

This handsome species has pale blue-gray leaves, flatter than most echeverias, which form a beautiful textural rosette. Long yellow stems of dainty red and yellow flowers appear in summer.

EUPHORBIA
Euphorbia species

TEMPERATURE 50–86°F (10–30°C)
LIGHT High/Bright indirect
HUMIDITY Low
CARE Easy
HEIGHT & SPREAD Up to 3 x 2ft
(90 x 60cm)
WARNING! The sap is toxic

To define the group of plants known as euphorbias is impossible, as it includes a vast number of disparate species of various sizes and shapes. Those grown as houseplants include the stocky African milk tree and many cactuslike plants, including the weird, leafless pencil cactus. These plants thrive in sun and tolerate periods of drought.

WATERING Water from spring to fall, allowing the top of the potting soil to dry out between waterings; in winter, keep the potting soil almost dry.

FEEDING Apply a half-strength balanced liquid fertilizer once a month from spring to fall.

PLANTING AND CARE Plant in a pot that fits the root ball in cactus potting soil (or a 2:1 mix of aerated potting soil and horticultural hard sand). Set in high light. Wear gloves when handling plants—the sap is a skin irritant. Repot every 2-3 years.

Euphorbia tirucalli

The pencil cactus looks like a deciduous shrub in winter. Its small foliage soon drops off to reveal a gaunt silhouette of smooth, tactile stems.

Euphorbia enopla

Disguised as a cactus, the pincushion euphorbia plant produces ribbed gray-green branched stems up to 12in (30cm) in height, covered in red spines.

Euphorbia trigona

The African milk tree's impressive, spiny, dark green stems mimic those of a cactus. The fingerlike leaves which sprout from them add to its appeal.

CHIHUAHUA FLOWER
Graptopetalum bellum

TEMPERATURE 50–80°F (10–27°C)
LIGHT High/Bright indirect
HUMIDITY Low
CARE Easy
HEIGHT & SPREAD 6 x 4in (15 x 10cm)

This little plant's tight rosette of white-rimmed, gray leaves might not look like much to write home about, but that all changes when the showy flowers make their appearance. The starry pink blooms, which are said to resemble little dogs' faces, shoot out from the center of the rosette on long, branched stems like tiny fireworks. Group a few together on a sunny shelf to intensify the effect.

WATERING Water from spring to fall, allowing the top of the potting soil to dry out between waterings; in winter, water just enough to prevent the potting soil from completely drying out.

FEEDING Apply a half-strength balanced liquid fertilizer 2-3 times during the growing period from spring to fall.

PLANTING AND CARE Plant in a small 4–5in (10–12.5cm) pot in cactus potting soil (or a 2:1 mix of aerated potting soil and horticultural hard sand). Stand in high light, or bright indirect light close to a window. This plant grows slowly and will only need repotting every 3 years when root-bound.

HAWORTHIA
Haworthia attenuata 'Striata'

TEMPERATURE 54–79°F (12–26°C)
LIGHT High/Bright indirect
HUMIDITY Low
CARE Easy
HEIGHT & SPREAD Up to 8 x 6in (20 x 15cm)

The spiky stems of this succulent make a striking contrast with more rounded succulents as part of a windowsill display. Some sport white raised stripes or spotted reddish bumps, which add to haworthia's rich texture, while slender stems of long tubular white flowers may appear on mature plants in the summer.

WATERING From spring to fall, allow the top of the potting soil to dry out between waterings. In winter, water sparingly, just enough to prevent the potting soil from completely drying out.

FEEDING Apply a half-strength balanced liquid fertilizer once a month from spring to fall.

PLANTING AND CARE Grow in a small 3–4in (7.5–10cm) pot in cactus potting soil (or a 2:1 mix of aerated potting soil and horticultural hard sand). Set in high or bright indirect light, on or close to a windowsill. Repot every 2–3 years in spring, but only when root-bound.

KALANCHOE
Kalanchoe blossfeldiana AGM

TEMPERATURE 54–80°F (12–26°C)
LIGHT High/Bright indirect
HUMIDITY Low
CARE Easy
HEIGHT & SPREAD 18 x 12in (45 x 30cm)
WARNING! All parts toxic to pets

Kalanchoe's heads of bright flowers appear in spring and summer, creating a show of color against the round, fleshy green leaves. The red, pink, or white blooms often last up to 12 weeks, but plants are reluctant to reflower, so you may need to replace them each year.

WATERING From spring to summer, water from the bottom when the top of the potting soil feels dry, ensuring the leaves do not get wet, as this can cause rot. Keep the potting soil almost dry through fall and winter.

FEEDING Apply a half-strength balanced liquid fertilizer every 2 weeks from spring to summer.

PLANTING AND CARE Grow in a 4–6in (10–15cm) pot in cactus potting soil (or a 2:1 mix of aerated potting soil and horticultural hard sand). Cut the flower stems down after blooming. Repot every year in a container one size larger, or buy new plants annually.

FLOWER DUST PLANT
Kalanchoe pumila

TEMPERATURE 50–80°F (10–27°C)
LIGHT High/Bright indirect
HUMIDITY Low
CARE Easy
HEIGHT & SPREAD 18 x 18in (45 x 45cm)
WARNING! All parts toxic to pets

There are many types of kalanchoe, but if you have space for only one, this should be at the top of your list. The powdery-white leaves have serrated edges that look like they have been cut with pinking shears, and in summer it bursts into bloom, bearing clusters of small, starry pink flowers on slim stems.

WATERING From spring to summer, water from the bottom when the top of the potting soil feels dry; keep the potting soil almost dry through fall and winter.

FEEDING Apply a half-strength balanced liquid fertilizer every month from spring to late summer.

PLANTING AND CARE Plant in a 4–6in (10–15cm) pot in cactus potting soil (or a 2:1 mix of aerated potting soil and horticultural hard sand). Stand in high light, and in a room with good ventilation. Repot every 2–3 years in spring when root-bound.

PANDA PLANT
Kalanchoe tomentosa

TEMPERATURE 60–75°F (15–23°C)
LIGHT High/Bright indirect
HUMIDITY Low
CARE Easy
HEIGHT & SPREAD Up to 2 x 2ft
(60 x 60cm)
WARNING! All parts toxic to pets

The gray, velvety leaves, with brown spots along the edges, give this curious succulent a tactile quality and its name. Grown for its foliage, it can form quite a large plant with a treelike silhouette, but it is unlikely to flower indoors.

WATERING From spring to summer, water from the bottom when the top of the potting soil feels dry, ensuring the leaves do not get wet. Keep the potting soil almost dry through fall and winter.

FEEDING Apply a half-strength balanced liquid fertilizer every month from spring to late summer.

PLANTING AND CARE Plant in cactus potting soil (or a 2:1 mix of aerated potting soil and horticultural hard sand) in a 4–8in (10–20cm) pot. Stand in high light in a room with good ventilation. Repot every 3 years in spring when root-bound.

LIVING STONE
Lithops species

TEMPERATURE 65–78°F (18–26°C)
LIGHT High
HUMIDITY Low
CARE Easy
HEIGHT & SPREAD 5ft x 2ft 6in
(1.5 x 0.75m)

The leafless stems of these South African natives look little flat-topped stones. Choose from plain gray-green types, or those with spotted and patterned foliage. In fall, a white, daisylike flower may grow from the crease in the top of the stem. Fun for children, these plants require little attention and are very easy to grow.

WATERING From winter to late summer, water only when the leaves start to shrivel; water slightly more in fall, so that the leaves remain firm.

FEEDING Apply a quarter-strength balanced liquid fertilizer once in fall.

PLANTING AND CARE Grow in a small 3–4in (7.5–10cm) pot in cactus potting soil (or a 2:1 mix of aerated potting soil and horticultural hard sand). Set in high light, especially in winter, when it will continue to grow. These plants can stay in the same pot for many years and prefer their own small, individual containers. Repot in late winter, just before you resume watering it more frequently.

MOONSTONES
Pachyphytum oviferum

TEMPERATURE 50–80°F (10–27°C)
LIGHT High
HUMIDITY Low
CARE Easy
HEIGHT & SPREAD 4 x 12in
(10 x 30cm)
WARNING! All parts toxic to pets

These tiny succulents look like a handful of beach pebbles planted in a pot, and are guaranteed to create a talking point, despite their diminutive size. The plump round leaves are pale blue-green to blue-purple, and in winter, the plant looks even more bizarre, when stems up to 12in (30cm) long appear, topped with dangling orange-red flowers.

WATERING Allow the soil to dry out before watering, and avoid getting water on the leaves. In winter, give a little more water, as this is when the plant grows.

FEEDING Apply a quarter-strength balanced liquid fertilizer once in winter, although it will not suffer if not fed at all.

PLANTING AND CARE Grow in a small 3–4in (7.5–10cm) pot in cactus potting soil (or a 2:1 mix of aerated potting soil and horticultural hard sand). Set in high light, especially in winter when it is in growth. Only repot when the plant is root-bound, after it has flowered.

HOUSELEEK
Sempervivum species

TEMPERATURE 50–80°F (-14–27°C)
LIGHT High/Bright indirect
HUMIDITY Low
CARE Easy
HEIGHT & SPREAD Up to 8 x 12in (20 x 30cm)

The spiraling leaves of this tiny succulent come in a huge range of colors, including all shades of green, red, burgundy, and gray. Many sport tempting variegations, and some are covered in fine hairs. Starry flowers appear on stout stems in summer.

WATERING Allow the top of the potting soil to dry out between waterings from spring to fall; water once a month in winter.

FEEDING Apply a half-strength balanced liquid fertilizer once a month from spring to fall.

PLANTING AND CARE Plant in a 2:1 mix of aerated potting soil and sand in a 3–4in (7.5–10cm) pot. Stand in high light. The leaf rosette dies after flowering, but new baby plants appear to replace the old ones. Repot every 2–3 years when root-bound.

DONKEY'S TAIL
Sedum morganianum

TEMPERATURE 50–80°F (10–27°C)
LIGHT High/Bright indirect
HUMIDITY Low
CARE Easy
HEIGHT & SPREAD 4 x 12in (10 x 30cm)

This Mexican native has great appeal, its ropelike stems of tiny round leaves creating an amazing textural effect. It makes a great focal point on a shelf or windowsill, but handle the plant with care, as the leaves are brittle and break off easily. The small flowers, which form at the tips of the stems, rarely appear on plants grown indoors.

WATERING Allow the top of the potting soil to dry out between waterings from spring to fall; water once a month in winter.

FEEDING Apply a half-strength balanced liquid fertilizer once a month from spring to fall.

PLANTING AND CARE Grow in a small 4–6in (10–15cm) pot in cactus potting soil (or a 2:1 mix of aerated potting soil and horticultural hard sand). Stand in a bright spot, but out of strong midday sun in summer. Repot every 2–3 years in spring, only when root-bound.

TEMPERATURE 60–75°F (15–24°C)
LIGHT Bright indirect
HUMIDITY High
CARE Easy
HEIGHT & SPREAD 4 x 18in (10 x 45cm)

The foliage of these pocket-sized plants ranges from silvery and spiky, to curled and spidery. Most flower annually, and the blooms are often surprisingly large and colorful. Plants die after flowering but, like all bromeliads, baby plants form to replace the old ones (see pp.206–07).

WATERING Place in a tray of lukewarm unsoftened water for 30 minutes to 1 hour once a week, then remove from the tray and let drain (see p.185). Avoid wetting the flowers by propping up the air plants.

FEEDING Mist with a special *Tillandsia* fertilizer once a month.

PLANTING AND CARE Display plants in glass jars or shells, or on driftwood, bark, or a decorative tray. Do not use glue. Keep in a humid area out of direct sun and away from heaters.

AIR PLANTS

These tiny treasures can literally be grown in thin air, requiring no sand or potting soil to put on a performance. Plants come in a wide range of shapes and sizes; some resemble little sea urchins, while others look more like conventional bromeliads (see pp.102–05), the family to which air plants belong. When mature, these beauties will burst into bloom, brightening up your home with exotic, colorful flowers. Few plants are easier to care for, so if you are a beginner, they will not disappoint.

Tillandsia aeranthos

This air plant flowers reliably every year, with pink and purple blooms appearing between a spray of stiff green leaves.

AIR PLANTS
Tillandsia species and hybrids

Tillandsia argentea AGM

The thin, spiky foliage of this tiny species radiates out from the center, resembling a sea urchin. Mature plants also bear a long, slim, red flowerhead, which holds tiny purple blooms that are guaranteed to turn heads.

Tillandsia cyanea

One of the most popular air plants, the pink quill, as it is commonly known, has dark green strappy leaves and an oval-shaped flowerhead, made up of pink bracts (petal-like modified leaves) and small, violet-blue flowers.

Tillandsia tenuifolia

This air plant soon forms a clump of spiky green foliage, and it will also tolerate a little neglect, quickly reviving after watering. The pink flower spikes resemble shooting stars and terminate in a cluster of tubular violet blooms.

Tillandsia bulbosa

Like a spider with curled legs, the long, thin foliage of this unusual air plant grows from a bulblike center, from which tubular pink and purple flowers emerge in early spring. The foliage also turns red when the buds form.

Tillandsia juncea

Small and compact, the silver grassy foliage of this elegant air plant is prone to drying out, so water it regularly every week. The blooms look like rows of tiny violet and pink lipsticks when they emerge from the narrow flower spike.

Tillandsia xerographica

The silver foliage of this must-have plant sprawls and curls to form a dense clump. As it requires less water than most, mist regularly rather than soaking. The long-lasting spike of violet blooms only appears on mature plants.

CARE AND CULTIVATION

BUYING A NEW
HOUSEPLANT

It's easy to get carried away when looking around a plant store or nursery. So, before you hand over your money, take a look at these tips to make sure you buy strong, healthy plants that will thrive when you bring them home. Check out the tool kit, too (see right), and pick up anything you will need to care for your new purchases.

IN THE STORE

Take a shopping list of the plants you like with you and try to stick to it when you get to the nursery or garden center. If, when you arrive, you fall in love with a plant that is not on your list, check the plant label carefully or ask the nursery staff first before buying to make sure you can give it the conditions it needs. If you are sure you will be able to look after it well, give your chosen plant a thorough health check (see right) and look at its base to see whether its pot has drainage holes. If not, repot it when you get home, as a lack of drainage frequently leads to waterlogging and fungal diseases.

GIVE YOUR PLANTS A HEALTH CHECK

Inspect any potential purchase carefully using this checklist, and reject any that show signs of pests or diseases (see pp.214–19).

1 Check for signs of wilting, which may be a sign of root pests.

2 Look out for dark spots or streaks on the leaves, stems, or flowers that could indicate disease or a virus.

3 Inspect the undersides of leaves and stems for pests or pest damage.

4 Check the potting soil for pests.

5 Tip the plant out of its pot (if you can) and check that it is not root-bound.

TAKING YOUR PLANT HOME

Depending on where you live, you may need to protect tender plants from the cold in winter by wrapping them in plastic. Do not expose them to temperatures below freezing, even for just a short time, as this could prove fatal for tender types. If the odd leaf or flower stem is damaged during the journey home, cut it off down to healthy growth or the base of the plant to prevent diseases entering through the wounds.

AT HOME

Unwrap the plant, repot it if necessary (see left), then place it, still in its plastic pot, in a waterproof container (sometimes referred to as a "cachepot" or "sleeve") or on a tray. Give the plant a good drink (see pp.184–87) and leave it to drain. Finally, check the plant's other care requirements (see the Plant Profiles chapter, pp.100–75) and place it in a suitable spot that provides the optimum light and temperature for it to thrive.

Check for drainage holes
Make sure the plant's pot has adequate drainage to prevent it from rotting. If it does not, repot it when you get home.

HOUSEPLANT TOOL KIT

With the tools and materials below, you will be fully equipped to care for the vast majority of houseplants.

Small watering can with rose attachment for watering from above

Decorative waterproof pots and drip trays for drainage

Dibble for making holes in potting soil for seeds and seedlings

Small trowel for tiny pots

Pebbles

Narrow trowel for larger plants

Mister spray

Small sharp knife

Garden scissors for pruning

Small hand fork

Brush for removing potting soil from cacti and delicate plants

Soft cloth to wipe leaves

GET THE
LIGHT RIGHT

Providing your plant with the amount of light it needs is essential for its long-term health. Sun supplies plants with energy—too little may inhibit their ability to flower, while too much can scorch the leaves or lead to wilting, so assess the light levels in your home to find the ideal positions for your plants.

CHOOSING THE PERFECT SPOT

Whether you live in a bright house with windows on all sides or in a small flat that receives little or no direct sunlight, there is a range of plants to suit your situation. Use this floorplan to help you identify what light levels you have in your living space, so that you can choose the best plants to match those conditions. Remember to take into account neighboring buildings or tall trees that may cast additional shade throughout the day, and bear in mind that light levels may fluctuate over the course of the year, depending on the season.

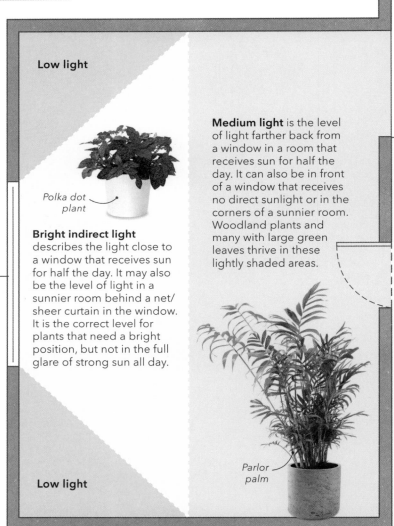

Low light

Window with direct sun for half the day

Polka dot plant

Bright indirect light describes the light close to a window that receives sun for half the day. It may also be the level of light in a sunnier room behind a net/ sheer curtain in the window. It is the correct level for plants that need a bright position, but not in the full glare of strong sun all day.

Medium light is the level of light farther back from a window in a room that receives sun for half the day. It can also be in front of a window that receives no direct sunlight or in the corners of a sunnier room. Woodland plants and many with large green leaves thrive in these lightly shaded areas.

Low light

Parlor palm

Find your light levels ▲
This floorplan shows a home with windows on three sides of the building, each letting in different levels of light, as described in the Plant Profiles chapter (pp.100–75). Note that one room may receive up to three different levels of sunlight.

Front door with small window

**Window with
no direct sunlight**

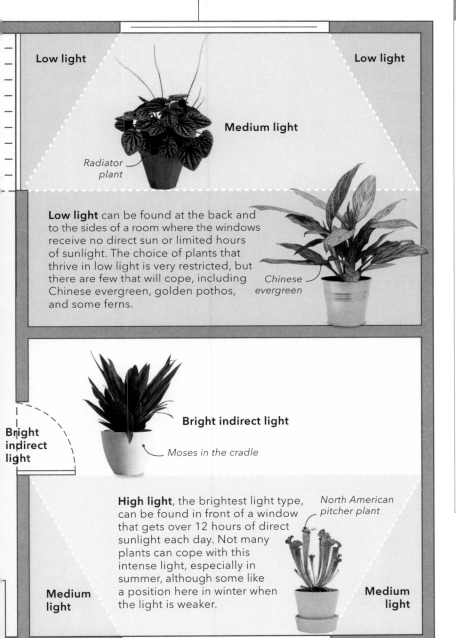

Low light

Low light

Medium light

*Radiator
plant*

Low light can be found at the back and
to the sides of a room where the windows
receive no direct sun or limited hours
of sunlight. The choice of plants that
thrive in low light is very restricted, but
there are few that will cope, including
Chinese evergreen, golden pothos,
and some ferns.

*Chinese
evergreen*

Bright
indirect
light

Bright indirect light

Moses in the cradle

High light, the brightest light type,
can be found in front of a window
that gets over 12 hours of direct
sunlight each day. Not many
plants can cope with this
intense light, especially in
summer, although some like
a position here in winter when
the light is weaker.

*North American
pitcher plant*

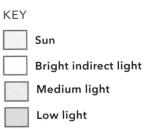

Medium
light

Medium
light

**Window with direct sunlight
for most of the day**

TIPS FOR INCREASING LIGHT LEVELS

1 Clean leaves regularly to increase
the amount of light that reaches
your plant. Use a soft, damp cloth
to remove dust every week, taking
care not to damage the foliage.

2 Turn your plants by 90 degrees
every few days so that each side
receives sufficient sun and grows
evenly, no matter what light levels
your living space receives. This
will prevent the plant becoming
misshapen over time (see p.213).

3 Take note of light variations
between seasons. In localities with
marked seasons, sunlight is stronger
in summer and weaker in winter,
when the days are also shorter. In
these areas, plants that like bright
indirect light may need to be set
closer to a sunny window in winter. If
this is the case, take care not to leave
them trapped behind curtains on a
cold windowsill at night, as the
extreme drop in temperature could
cause them harm.

4 Boost low light levels in your
living space using artificial lights
(also known as "grow lights"),
which imitate the sun's rays. There
is a range of easy-to-install units
suitable for the home gardener;
always ask the supplier's advice
before buying, as some may emit
too much or too little light for the
plants you wish to grow.

KEY

☐ Sun

☐ Bright indirect light

☐ Medium light

☐ Low light

CHECK THE
TEMPERATURE

While most houseplants will grow quite happily in our warm homes, they may suffer in extremely hot or cold spots. Check your plants' preferred temperatures (see pp.100–75) and use the advice below to find the perfect spot to display them.

"Keep tropical plants away from heat sources and drafty areas."

PROVIDE OPTIMUM TEMPERATURES

While many houseplants will cope with a relatively wide temperature range, always check your plant's specific needs in the Plant Profiles chapter (see pp.100–75). As many houseplants come from tropical areas, few will be able to deal with long periods of very low temperatures. Equally, extended hot spells could cause some plants to dehydrate quickly and wilt. If you have a plant that you cannot identify, the safest range is between 54–75°F (12–24°C), which suits the majority of houseplants.

Drafty hallways will suit a few woodland plants, such as the button fern, and tough types like golden pothos and the umbrella plant. Other plants, including most tropical varieties, should be kept elsewhere, in areas where temperatures are consistently warmer.

Hot, dry areas near open fires or heaters are not suitable for any houseplants, so keep them at a safe distance.

Button fern

Lady palm

Away from the window, temperatures will be more even throughout the day, which will suit plants that also prefer lower-light conditions.

Find the right temperature ▶
Use this illustration to identify different sources of heat and drafts and find the best locations to display your plants.

NORMAL TEMPERATURE VARIATIONS

All plants are adapted to deal with some fluctuations in temperature, but these should not fall below or exceed its minimum or maximum temperature requirements for long periods (see Plant Profiles, pp.100–75), as this could harm the plant (see p.213).

Day-to-night temperature drops of about 9–18°F (5–10°C) are normal for most plants, as that is what they would experience in nature. However, some plants, such as cymbidium orchids (see right), will only form flowers when there is a drop of more than 18°F (10°C) at night (see p.197).

Seasonal temperature variations can be felt by most plants, even inside our heated homes, and in winter, this often leads to a reduction in growth. Some plants have adapted to cold climates by becoming dormant in winter; these will need to be moved to an unheated area at this time of year.

Cymbidium orchid

Heat rises, meaning that rooms will be warmer closer to the ceiling. Water hanging plants more frequently than others in the same room.

Lipstick plant

The ideal spot for most houseplants is an area a short distance from sunny windows and away from heaters.

Angel wings

Rex begonias

Windowsills can fluctuate a lot in temperature, even those beside double-glazed windows. They can become extremely warm in summer and chilly during the winter. On hot days, open windows or turn on the air conditioning to keep the room cool, and do not trap plants between the window and curtains at night in winter.

HOW TO WATER YOUR
HOUSEPLANTS

Watering most houseplants can be pretty straightforward, provided you understand their individual needs. By following a few simple rules, you can make sure that they receive just the right amount of moisture to keep them thriving.

WHEN TO WATER

Most houseplants prefer moist potting soil in spring and summer when they are in growth, but take care not to water too much; soggy, waterlogged potting soil causes disease and can be fatal, while a little drought is easily remedied. To prevent wet potting soil, keep your plants in pots with drainage holes at the bottom, so that any excess water can drain out, and tip away any surplus that is sitting in the plant's decorative cachepot or tray about an hour after watering.

HOW TO WATER

To keep your plants in peak condition, check the specific advice for each one in the Plant Profiles chapter (see pp.100–75) and use the watering method (or methods) appropriate to your plant, as outlined in the five options on the right.

THE GOLDEN RULES OF WATERING

1 Keep plants in pots with drainage holes to prevent waterlogging.

2 Water most plants every 2–4 days (or as required) in spring and summer to keep the soil moist (not waterlogged).

3 Water desert cacti and succulents less frequently (only when the top of the potting soil feels dry).

4 Reduce frequency of watering in winter when plant growth is slower and temperatures are lower.

5 Tip out excess water from cachepots and trays to prevent overly soggy potting soil.

6 Avoid getting water on the leaves and stems of plants with soft, furry foliage, or succulents and cacti.

7 Check the Plant Profiles chapter (see pp.100–75) to see if your plant prefers unsoftened water.

Watering from above
Pour water from above if your plant is happy for its foliage to be doused; most tropical plants and ferns are in this category. Make sure that the potting soil is also soaked, or you risk watering the leaves without any moisture reaching the roots.

Watering from below
Set your plant in a pot with drainage holes in a tray of water about ¾in (2cm) deep. Leave for 20 minutes, then remove and drain. Use this method for plants that do not like wet leaves or stems, such as African violets, or if foliage is covering the potting soil.

"Take care not to overwater your plants; soggy potting soil will harm them far more quickly than drought."

MOISTURE LEVELS EXPLAINED

Almost dry potting soil should feel dry ¾in (2cm) beneath the surface, but may be slightly damp lower down. Most succulents and cacti require their soil to be this dry between waterings.

A dry top layer of potting soil should feel dry to the touch on the surface. Many plants should feel dry before water is reapplied; others may only need this level of moisture in winter when growth is slow.

Moist potting soil should feel damp to touch, but not look wet and glistening. Make sure the plant pot has drainage holes, and tip out any excess water about an hour after watering.

Wet potting soil should be entirely soaked and have a glistening surface. Carnivorous plants are among the few that require this. Plant in a pot with drainage holes and stand in a tray of water.

STOP THE ROT

Drought-loving cacti and succulents like their leaves and stems to remain dry at all times, so add a layer of hard sand (known as a "mulch") on top of the potting soil if repotting. Mulch helps water to quickly drain away, preventing them from rotting.

Misting leaves and aerial roots
Some plants absorb moisture through their leaves and aerial roots. Examples include orchids, mandevillas, and lady palms. Mist the leaves and roots regularly, but also water the potting soil to keep them healthy.

Watering bromeliads
The leaves and bracts (petal-like modified leaves) of most bromeliads form a cuplike reservoir in the center of the plant. Fill this up with unsoftened water, replenishing it every few weeks. Also water the potting soil so that it is moist.

Soaking air plants
Air plants are best soaked in a tray of unsoftened water for an hour once a week. After soaking, leave to drain, and make sure they dry fully within 4 hours to prevent them rotting. Alternatively, mist them 2–3 times a week.

WATERING WHEN YOU GO AWAY

Most plants will survive a long weekend without any water, and many cacti and succulents will be fine for a couple of weeks if you bring them into a cool, bright room and give them a drink immediately on your return. For all other plants, you will need to take action. If you do not have a green-thumbed neighbor or friend who can water while you are away, try these simple tricks to keep your plants in good health.

"Use these clever tricks to keep your plants hydrated while you're away from home."

Water bottle method
Cut the bottom off a plastic water bottle and make a tiny hole in the cap with a tip of hot skewer. Screw the cap onto the bottle and push it into the potting soil. Fill the bottle with water; this will then drip slowly into the soil. Make sure the plant pot has drainage holes so that the soil does not become too wet.

The wick system
Stand a bowl of water on an upturned pot so that it is higher than the surface of the potting soil. Weigh down a strip of capillary matting (available from garden centers) in the bowl, then push the other end into the soil. The matting will slowly water the plant. This technique is the best option for watering single plants, or large plants that cannot be moved.

Easy sink method
Fill the kitchen sink with water and place either capillary matting or an old towel on the draining board, with one end in the water. Remove your plants from their cachepots and set them on the wet matting or towel, so that moisture can be drawn up through the drainage holes to the roots.

RAISING HUMIDITY LEVELS

The dry atmosphere in our homes can cause some plants' foliage to dry out and turn brown, inhibiting growth. The many houseplants that hail from the tropics are especially vulnerable, as they are adapted to thrive in humid air. Try to replicate this atmosphere in your home using one or two of the methods here.

Tray of wet pebbles
An easy way to raise humidity levels is to set your plant on a shallow tray filled with stone or hydroleca ceramic pebbles. Pour in water so it just covers the pebbles, and set your plant pot on top (not in the water). As the water gradually evaporates, it creates a humid atmosphere around the plant.

HUMIDITY LEVELS EXPLAINED

High humidity means that the air is saturated with moisture. Tropical plants thrive in this atmosphere, but they may be difficult to care for in homes with central heating (which can dry out the air). If you want to keep these demanding plants, place them in a humid area of your home, or invest in a room humidifier.

Moderate humidity is required by many houseplants, including orchids, ferns, some palms, and a large number of foliage plants. Misting them regularly, setting them on a tray of wet pebbles, and grouping a few together will help to raise the humidity to the correct level.

Low humidity is where the atmosphere holds little moisture. Plants from arid regions (such as cacti, succulents, and those from Mediterranean areas) are adapted to these conditions. Most rooms in centrally heated homes have low levels of air moisture, although drought-lovers will not cope well in humid rooms of the home.

Misting plants
Increase the humidity around your plant by misting the leaves and aerial roots every day or two; this also cleans the leaves. However, plants with fuzzy leaves or an infection should never be misted, and the benefits of misting can be short-lived. Check the advice for your chosen plants in the Plant Profiles chapter (see pp.100–75) to see whether misting is right for them.

Grouping plants
All plants release water through a process known as "transpiration," just like we do when we breathe out. You can create a tropical microclimate by grouping a few plants together, where each of them will benefit from the moisture released by their neighbors.

FEEDING
YOUR PLANTS

Put your houseplants on a diet of essential nutrients and they will reward you with healthy flowers and foliage. Like us, however, they can suffer if you feed them too much or too little. Knowing what to feed your plants, and how often, will help them stay on track.

"Fertilizer provides the nutrients plants would draw from the soil if planted outdoors."

FOOD ESSENTIALS

While most plants growing in the ground can get all the nutrients they need from the soil, plants in pots rely entirely on you for their food supply. Many potting soils contain fertilizers, but after your plant has used these up, you will have to step in and start feeding them. The type of fertilizer and dosage depends on the plant, so check its specific needs in the Plant Profiles chapter (pp.100–75).

Well-nourished plants
A well-fed plant will display vigorous growth and none of the tell-tale signs of over- or underfeeding, such as yellowing or pale leaves.

PLANT NUTRIENTS EXPLAINED

The main plant nutrients are nitrogen (N), phosphorus (P), and potassium (K). Balanced fertilizers contain all three nutrients, together with a range of trace elements that plants need in smaller quantities. The nutrient content of a fertilizer is often shown on the packaging as a ratio of N:P:K; a balanced fertilizer, for instance, would be 20:20:20. Most plants only need to be fed when they are actively growing, usually between spring and fall, and they require few or no extra nutrients in winter. Plants also take up fertilizer through their roots in a solution, so dry potting soil will not only dehydrate them but also limit their ability to absorb fertilizer.

Nitrogen (N) is known as the leaf-maker, because it promotes strong, healthy foliage. This in turn encourages good overall growth, since the foliage feeds the whole plant. It is particularly important for leafy houseplants.

Phosphorus (P) is the root-maker, and it is required by all plants to grow and develop. The roots transport food and water to the plant, thus enabling strong and healthy growth.

Potassium (K) is essential for the development of flowers and fruits. Fertilizers with a high potassium content are often given to plants a few months before they are due to bloom to encourage lots of buds to form.

CHOOSING A FERTILIZER

Different plants have different dietary needs, so make sure you are giving the correct fertilizer at the right dosage. Remember that overfeeding plants can be as bad, or worse, than underfeeding them (see p.213).

Balanced liquid fertilizer
The majority of houseplants need a balanced liquid fertilizer, which you can buy as either a powder or liquid that you then dilute, or as a ready-mixed solution. This type of fertilizer is applied at regular intervals throughout the growing season, usually from spring to fall.

High-potassium fertilizer
This fertilizer is rich in flower-promoting potassium (see opposite). It is usually sold as a liquid that you dilute before use. Tomato fertilizers have a high potassium content, and can be used on flowering plants, as well as those that produce fruits, such as the Jerusalem cherry.

Slow-release granular fertilizer
Large or woody plants, such as trees, shrubs, and perennial climbers, may benefit from an all-purpose granular fertilizer. Apply undiluted as granules or in tablet form (shown left) to the potting soil once a year, usually in early spring. Watering breaks down the granules, which then release their nutrients.

This bottle drip-feeds the orchid with a specially formulated fertilizer

Special houseplant fertilizer
Manufacturers have developed fertilizers that have been carefully formulated for plants with specific needs, such as orchids, cacti, and carnivorous plants. They are usually sold in simple-to-use solutions; some are supplied in small bottles that can be inserted into the potting soil, where they drip-feed nutrients to the plant over time (see above).

PICKING POTTING SOIL
FOR YOUR PLANTS

Use this guide to choose the best type of potting soil for your plant, and any additional materials you may need when potting it up. Always use fresh soil when repotting (see pp.192–93); do not reuse old soil from other plants, as this will lack nutrients and could also harbor hidden diseases or pests.

WHAT IS POTTING SOIL?

"Potting soil" (or, more accurately, "growing media") is the term commonly used to describe the medium that potted plants are grown in. There are many different types, made up of a combination of soil (or "loam"), decomposed organic matter (similar to the compost you may make at home in a compost bin), aggregates such as hard sand, and fertilizers. Some also contain peat, but because its extraction threatens the sustainability of natural peat bogs, many people prefer to use peat-free alternatives.

Multipurpose potting soil
Also known as all-purpose potting soil, this lightweight type is available with or without peat. Made from natural materials, such as coconut fiber, bark, and composted wood fiber, most also contain enough fertilizer to feed plants for a few weeks.
BEST FOR Annual flowering houseplants

Soil- or loam-based potting soil
This type contains sterilized soil, together with some of the natural materials in multipurpose potting soils and a range of essential plant nutrients. It is generally used for plants that will live in their pots for more than 1 year.
BEST FOR Trees, shrubs, and perennial climbers

Houseplant potting soil
Formulated to meet the needs of most houseplants, this offers a quick and easy solution if you do not know the needs of your plant. Similar to multipurpose potting soil, most types contain peat and a range of essential plant nutrients.
BEST FOR Most houseplants, except for those with special needs, such as orchids and cacti (see opposite)

Seed and cutting potting soil

As the name suggests, this is the best choice for sowing seeds and taking cuttings. It is free-draining to prevent rotting, and its fine texture means that even tiny seeds are in contact with the soil, aiding germination.

BEST FOR Sowing seeds; taking cuttings; potting up young seedlings

Special potting soils

Formulated for specific plant groups, such as orchids, cacti, or carnivorous plants, this range of soils takes the guesswork out of making your own mixes for plants that demand very particular conditions.

BEST FOR Orchids, cacti and succulents, carnivorous plants

Acidifying potting soil

Similar to multipurpose, this soil is designed for plants that require acidic soil conditions, such as azaleas and blue hydrangeas. After planting, remember to use a fertilizer for acid-loving plants when those in the soil have been used up.

BEST FOR Azaleas, blue hydrangeas, and some ferns

OTHER MATERIALS YOU MAY NEED

The following materials are often mixed with potting soil to lighten or aerate it, or to help increase drainage. Check the potting advice for your particular plant in the Plant Profiles chapter (pp.100–75) to see if it needs them, and the correct quantities to use.

Vermiculite and perlite are minerals that have been heated to produce spongy grains. Both increase drainage while retaining and holding water well, then releasing it slowly back into the soil. They are often mixed with potting soil or used to cover seeds to keep them moist.

Gravel and hard sand can both prevent soggy soil. Gravel, if added to the bottom of a pot, creates a reservoir that water can drain into, while smaller hard sand particles are often mixed with potting soil to increase drainage, providing ideal conditions for succulents and other drought-lovers.

Horticultural sand is often used in combination with potting soil to create the free-draining conditions succulents and other drought-loving plants need. Always use washed, sterilized, fine-grade sand; builders' sand contains too much lime for most houseplants.

Sphagnum moss can be placed on the surface of the soil to help create the moist conditions enjoyed by some plants, such as ferns. It is also included in the growing medium for carnivorous plants and a few other species that like wet or too-wet conditions.

POTS AND
REPOTTING

Choosing the right pot will help you to keep your houseplants healthy. A good container should offer plenty of drainage, and will need to be replaced every few years as the plant grows to avoid its roots becoming congested and "root-bound."

HOW TO TELL A PLANT NEEDS REPOTTING

Check the following factors, which can mean your plant needs repotting:

1 Waterlogged soil may indicate that the plant's pot has no drainage, in which case it needs a new one with drainage holes.

2 Roots are growing through the drainage holes at the bottom of the container, suggesting the plant is root-bound (also known as pot-bound).

3 The roots are tightly encircling the sides of the root ball when you tip it out. Note: some plants prefer their roots to be confined, so check the repotting advice for yours in the Plant Profiles chapter (see pp.100–75)

4 The leaves are pale or yellow, which may be a sign that the roots are congested and unable to take up nutrients efficiently.

5 The plant is wilting, which may also be a sign of congested roots.

HOW TO REPOT A PLANT

When repotting a plant, opt for a pot one size larger than the container in which it is currently housed, with drainage holes at the bottom to allow excess water to filter out. You can use either a decorative pot with drainage holes and a waterproof tray, as we have done here, or a plain plastic pot, which can then be hidden inside a prettier waterproof container, known as a "cachepot."

WHAT YOU WILL NEED

PLANT
- Root-bound plant

OTHER MATERIALS
- Pot one size larger than the original with drainage holes in the bottom
- Potting soil to suit the plant (see Plant Profiles, pp.100–75)
- Decorative waterproof container (optional)

TOOLS
- Watering can (fitted with a rose attachment if necessary)

1 Most plants are repotted every 2–3 years, or annually when they are young. If you suspect yours is root-bound, check to see if the roots are growing through the drainage holes of its pot.

2 Choose a new pot that is wide and deep enough to fit the root ball, with some space around the edges and at the top to allow for watering. Water the plant well about half an hour before repotting it.

"A root-bound plant will have tightly packed roots that are growing through its pot's drainage holes."

3 Add a layer of potting soil to the bottom of the new pot. Remove the plant from its original container. Gently tease out the roots that are tightly packed around the edges or at the bottom, and set the plant on the soil, checking that the top is sitting ½in (1cm) below the rim. This allows space for water to collect at the top before filtering into the potting soil.

4 Fill in around the roots with more potting soil, pressing it down gently to remove any air gaps. Do not bury the stems (or aerial roots, if it has any); it should be at the same depth as it was in its original pot. Water gently, taking care to keep the leaves dry.

CARING FOR LARGE PLANTS

If you have a large tree or shrub that you want to keep at the same size, try tipping it out of its container and lightly trimming off the roots around the sides, then return it to the same pot with fresh potting soil. Larger plants can also be kept in the same pot year after year if given a top dressing of fresh soil and fertilizer each spring—follow the steps to keep yours in good health.

1 Remove the top layer of potting soil, ensuring you do not damage the roots. Apply a slow-release fertilizer at the recommended rate (see p.189).

2 Add fresh soil to the same level as it was originally, patting it down to remove any air gaps. Water well to settle the new soil around the roots.

KEEPING YOUR PLANTS
IN SHAPE

If your plant has lost its shape, is threatening to outgrow its space, or has areas of dead or diseased growth, it needs a trim. Regular pruning can also encourage more flowers to form and make plants bushier, so follow these simple pruning techniques to keep your plants neat and in good health.

WHY PRUNE?

Keep a large plant compact
Removing or reducing long stems will help keep a plant's size in check, but pruning too frequently can actually stimulate growth, so cut it back just once or twice a year.

Remove dead or diseased parts
Cut out areas of the plant that look dead or diseased, and disinfect tools after use. Also remove stems that are rubbing against each other, which may cause abrasions.

Make a plant bushier
Removing the tips of a stem releases a chemical that stimulates the growth of more sideshoots lower down, and bushier growth. Use garden scissors or your fingers to nip out the tips.

Encourage more flowers
Deadhead your plants by taking out the old flowering stems after the blooms have faded. This diverts the plant's energy from making seeds into producing more flowers.

WHAT TO PRUNE

1 Dead, broken, or cracked stems

2 Diseased stems or any that are discolored or marked

3 Stems that are rubbing against one another

4 Brown or discolored leaves

5 Overly long stems that create a lopsided shape

6 Tips of stems, to encourage bushy growth

7 Leading stem(s) at the top of the plant, to prevent it from growing too tall

8 Old flowering stems, to encourage reflowering

9 Stems of plain-colored leaves on variegated plants

BEFORE

AFTER

HOW TO PRUNE

While you can cut back unhealthy growth at any time of year, most plants are best pruned during early spring, before they start a period of rapid growth; check the Plant Profiles chapter to confirm your plant's pruning needs (pp.100–75). Always check the plant before you begin so that you know which stems you will need to remove.

WHAT YOU WILL NEED

PLANTS
- Misshapen or large plant that has outgrown its space

TOOLS
- Sharp, clean garden scissors
- Household disinfectant

1 When pruning, use sharp garden scissors to cut just above a leaf stem, node (bump on the stem where new growth will develop), or side stem, where it meets the main stem. To take out a whole stem, remove it at the base.

2 Remove any dead, damaged, or diseased stems, cutting them back to healthy growth. Also cut out stems that are rubbing against one another. On variegated plants, remove any stems of plain, solid-colored leaves.

3 Once unhealthy growth is removed, reassess the plant's shape and cut away stems that are creating an awkward or lopsided shape. If there are gaps in the outline, prune the stem tips around them to encourage bushier growth.

4 If your plant is as tall as you want it to be, take out the leading stem to prevent further growth. When you have finished pruning your plant, clean your tools with household disinfectant, rinse them in the sink, and dry well.

HOW TO MAKE AN
ORCHID REFLOWER

Orchids are usually bought while flowering, and can bloom for many weeks if well cared for. When their flowers do eventually fade and die, encourage them to bloom again after a period of rest by following these simple steps.

BLOOMING HEALTH

The care needed to encourage an orchid to reflower will also keep your plant healthy, as you are offering the optimum conditions for it to thrive. A healthy orchid can live for decades and bloom every 8 to 12 months.

WHAT YOU WILL NEED

PLANT
- Mature orchid with fading flowers

OTHER MATERIALS
- Pot one size larger than the original with drainage holes in the bottom (optional)
- Potting soil to suit the plant (see Plant Profiles, pp.110–15)

TOOLS
- Garden scissors
- Soft cloth
- Watering can
- Mister spray or tray of wet pebbles
- Suitable fertilizer

1 Cut back the flowering stems to just above the second pale horizontal band. This allows the plant to put all its energy into making new leaves, rather than seed, which will supply energy for the next set of flowers.

2 Ensure the plant receives plenty of light, as too little sun will inhibit flower formation. Bring it closer to a window during winter, when the light is weaker, and dust the leaves every week or two to maximize the amount of light they can absorb. Remember to move the plant back out of direct midday sun during summer.

3 Repot the plant if it is tightly root-bound (see pp.192–93). Use a pot just one size larger than the original, as most orchids prefer slightly cramped roots.

4 Keep your plant hydrated as necessary, watering less frequently during winter. Mist the leaves and aerial roots every day or two with unsoftened water, or set on a tray of wet pebbles (see p.187).

5 Apply a special orchid or balanced liquid fertilizer, using the correct dosage for your plant (see pp.188–89). During winter, either fertilize the plant less or do not fertilize it at all, depending on its particular needs.

6 Check your plant's temperature needs, including if it requires a marked drop at night. After 9–12 months (depending on the type of orchid; see pp.110–15), move it to a cooler room to encourage buds to form, then bring it back into the warmth to bloom.

KNOW YOUR ORCHID'S NEEDS

Each type of orchid requires slightly different conditions to thrive and reflower, so check yours in the Orchids section of the Plant Profiles chapter (see pp.110–15) and tailor your care accordingly.

1 Take seasonal variations into consideration. Some orchids from cool, humid forests like lower temperatures, while others, such as moth orchids, flower well in warmer conditions.

2 Look out for orchids that need a marked difference between day and night temperatures to form flowers; *Cattleya*, *Cymbidium*, *Dendrobium nobile*, and *Vanda* all fall into this category.

3 Check if your plant needs a high-potassium fertilizer instead of a special orchid fertilizer to flower.

4 Be patient. While moth orchids could reflower after a dormancy of just 8 months, most orchids will only bloom once a year.

HOW TO GROW
BULBS INDOORS

Plant bulbs in fall for beautiful floral houseplant displays in winter and early spring. In cooler localities, tender bulbs, such as amaryllis, should be grown indoors, while hardy outdoor types can be "forced" to flower earlier inside by growing them in a cool spot, then moving them to a warmer room to bloom.

GROWING TENDER BULBS

Amaryllis bulbs (available from late fall to midwinter) are tender and will die in frosty conditions outside, but they can be planted indoors where, with a little care, they will grow into beautiful houseplants.

WHAT YOU WILL NEED

PLANTS
- Amaryllis bulb

OTHER MATERIALS
- Pot with drainage holes, slightly wider and about one and a half times as deep as the bulb
- Specially formulated potting soil for growing bulbs or multipurpose potting soil

TOOLS
- Watering can

1 Soak the bulb for a few hours. Set the bulb on a layer of potting soil, then fill in around it with more soil, leaving up to two-thirds of the bulb showing above the surface.

2 Water well and leave to drain. Stand the pot in a bright, warm place. Water sparingly until shoots appear; then keep the potting soil consistently moist.

3 Turn the pot every day so that stems grow evenly. Move to a cooler room where flower buds will appear 6–8 weeks after planting, and stake the tall stems, if necessary. After blooming, apply a balanced liquid fertilizer to the plant weekly until the leaves die down. Keep in a cool, bright position, and do not fertilize or water when dormant, from late summer to midfall.

GROWING HARDY BULBS

Outdoor bulbs are often "forced" to bloom earlier indoors than they would normally develop outside in the cold. Suitable bulbs include scented hyacinths (shown here) and grape hyacinths; daffodils and lilies of the valley require slightly different forcing methods (see below). Some bulbs, including hyacinths and paperwhite daffodils, will be labeled "prepared." These have been chilled to imitate a winter season, which they need to go through before flowering, and will bloom in winter rather than spring. Other bulbs do not require this treatment to flower earlier indoors, but may not bloom until late winter.

WHAT YOU WILL NEED

PLANTS
- Prepared hyacinth bulbs or unprepared grape hyacinth bulbs

OTHER MATERIALS
- Wide pot with drainage holes
- Bulb soil

TOOLS
- Gloves
- Black plastic bag
- Watering can with a rose attachment

1 Place a layer of bulb soil in a pot. Water and leave to drain. Wearing gloves (the bulbs can cause skin irritation), space the bulbs evenly on the soil, making sure the pointed ends face up.

2 Fill in around the bulbs with soil so the tips are just above the surface. Leave a ½in (1cm) gap between the soil and top of the pot. Place the pot in a black plastic bag and set in a cool, dark place.

3 Check every week and water lightly if the bulb soil is dry. When shoots are 2in (5cm) tall (usually 6–10 weeks later), remove the bag and bring the pot indoors into a cool room out of direct sun. Stand in a slightly warmer spot to flower.

FORCING DAFFODILS AND LILIES OF THE VALLEY

To force daffodil bulbs, follow steps 1 and 2 above, but cover the bulbs with a thin layer of potting soil. Set in a cool room below 50°F (10°C) for 6–12 weeks in a bright spot out of direct sun, then in a warmer area to flower. The best scented daffodils for forcing are tender paperwhites, which flower within 12 weeks.

Grow lilies of the valley from rhizomes, known as "pips," which are sold in winter with the roots already growing. Soak the pips for 2 hours, then plant in multipurpose potting soil in tall, deep pots with drainage holes, so the top of the pips are just below the surface. Water and leave in a cool room in medium light, out of direct sun. Flowers will appear 3–5 weeks later.

HOW TO PROPAGATE PLANTS

Filling your home with the plants you love can be expensive, but many are easy to propagate, giving you lots of new plants from your original purchase. Use the guide below to decide which method suits your plants best; many can be propagated from cuttings, while others are better grown from divisions, offsets, or seed.

WHICH PROPAGATION METHOD SHOULD I USE?

The stem cutting method suits most soft-stemmed plants; woodier stems can also be used, but may take longer to root. **(pp.200-01)**

The leaf cutting method is most effective for begonias, Cape primroses, snake plants, and succulents. **(pp.202-03)**

The water method will work for most houseplants, although woodier-stemmed plants may take longer to root. **(p.204)**

The division method can be used on plants with fibrous root systems that throw up new shoots next to the parent plant. **(p.205)**

The offset method suits plants which produce "baby" offsets, such as bromeliads and spider plants. **(pp.206-07)**

The seed method is most often used to grow annual plants; perennials can be sown, too, but may take longer to mature. **(pp.208-09)**

PROPAGATE FROM STEM CUTTINGS

One of the easiest ways to make new plants, this method is suitable for most soft-stemmed houseplants. Take your cuttings in spring or early summer, when the plant is growing quickly, and use young, pliable stems rather than older, woodier growth, which may take longer to root. Many plants, including this silver inch plant, will produce rooted cuttings in 6–8 weeks.

WHAT YOU WILL NEED

PLANT
- Mature plant with healthy young stems

OTHER MATERIALS
- Hormone rooting powder (optional)
- Small plastic pots or seed tray
- Cuttings potting soil
- Multipurpose potting soil

TOOLS
- Garden scissors or sharp, clean knife
- Dibble
- Small watering can fitted with a rose attachment
- Plastic bag and rubber band or clear seed tray or pot lid

1 In spring or early summer, select a nonflowering stem from a healthy plant. Using sharp garden scissors, cut off a 4–6in (10–15cm) section from the tip, just below a leaf joint.

2 Remove the lower 2–3 leaves (or sets of leaves, if they are opposite each other). Take a few cuttings using this method, making sure you leave plenty of stems on the parent plant.

3 Dip the end of each cutting into hormone rooting powder. This is an optional step, as most stems will produce roots without it, but they may take longer.

4 Fill a small plastic pot or seed tray with cuttings potting soil. With a dibble, make a hole in the soil. Place the cutting into the hole and firm around it gently.

5 Insert up to 3 cuttings per pot, or plant 6 in a small seed tray. Settle the soil around the stems by watering lightly with a watering can fitted with a rose attachment.

6 Cover the pot with a plastic bag secured with a rubber band or a tray lid. Keep the potting soil moist but not wet. Roots will develop in 6–8 weeks. When new shoots appear, transplant the cuttings into small pots of multipurpose potting soil. Set in a bright spot out of direct sun to grow on.

PROPAGATE FROM
LEAF CUTTINGS

It may seem unlikely that a leaf can produce roots, but many plants will perform this trick. Begonias, like the *Rex* begonia shown here, are the most frequently used for leaf cuttings, but you can also try Cape primroses, the snake plant, and succulents, such as *Kalanchoe* and *Echeveria*. These other plants require slightly different methods (see opposite).

WHAT YOU WILL NEED

PLANT
- Mature plant with large, healthy leaves

OTHER MATERIALS
- Cuttings potting soil
- Perlite

TOOLS
- Sharp knife or garden scissors
- Cutting board
- 5in (12cm) plastic pots or small seed tray
- Clear plastic bags and rubber bands
- Small watering can with a rose attachment
- Small pots
- Spoon
- Multipurpose potting soil

1 Select a healthy, mature plant with plenty of large leaves. Water it well about 30 minutes before taking your cuttings.

2 Select a large leaf and, using a sharp knife, remove it at the base of the leaf stem. Place on a clean cutting board.

3 Cut out a small circular section around the stem and discard. Divide the leaf into sections about ¾in (2cm) long, each with veins running through them (veins may be more visible on the reverse).

4 Fill a small pot or seed tray with cuttings potting soil and a handful of perlite. Press down gently to remove any air pockets. Carefully push the leaf segments in so they are standing up with the veins in contact with the soil.

6 Seal the pot with a plastic bag secured with a rubber band and leave in a warm area out of direct sun. Cuttings take about 6–8 weeks to form new leaves and roots. When 2–4 leaves emerge, use a spoon to remove each cutting, keeping the roots intact, and transfer into small pots of multipurpose potting soil. Water well, and set in a spot out of direct sun to grow on.

5 Using a small can fitted with a rose attachment, water the cuttings to help to settle the soil around them. Ensure excess water drains away, or the cuttings could rot.

LEAF CUTTING METHODS FOR OTHER PLANTS

Cape primrose leaves should be cut on either side of the midrib vein. Discard the midrib, and insert each side of the leaf into cuttings soil with the cut side down. Then follow steps 4 and 5.

Snake plants can be propagated by cutting a young, healthy leaf horizontally into 2in (5cm) sections. Take each of the sections and plant the edge that was closest to the base of the original leaf into cuttings soil. Then follow steps 4 and 5.

Succulent leaves should be kept whole and set aside for 24–48 hours until the cut ends dry out. Insert these ends into pots filled with a 2:1 mix of cactus potting soil and sand, then add some hard sand on top. Do not cover the cuttings. When new leaves have emerged, plant them into small pots of cactus soil, water lightly, and place in a bright position to grow on.

PROPAGATE WITH **WATER**

Quick and easy to do, this is a great propagation method for beginners. It is also fun for children, as they can watch the roots developing on the cut stems day by day. A large number of houseplants can be increased in this way, especially those with soft, pliable stems, such as the African violet (used here), golden pothos, and species of *Peperomia* and *Pilea*.

WHAT YOU WILL NEED

PLANT
- Mature, healthy plant

OTHER MATERIALS
- Multipurpose potting soil

TOOLS
- Scissors; sharp, clean knife; or garden scissors
- Glass or jar
- Small pots with drainage holes

1 Choose a healthy nonflowering stem and remove it at the base with a knife, scissors, or garden scissors. Cut the stem below a node (bump on the stem) if there is one.

2 Ensure the leaf has a clear portion of stem at least 2in (5cm) long. If the stem has a number of leaves growing from it, remove the bottom sets to leave the lower stem clear.

3 Place the cutting in a glass of water, ensuring the leaf or leaves are not submerged; rest them on the sides. After a few weeks, roots will grow from the base of the stem.

4 When a good root system has developed in the water, transplant each cutting into a small pot of multipurpose potting soil. Grow in a bright area out of direct sunlight.

PROPAGATE BY
DIVIDING PLANTS

Some plant varieties produce a network of fibrous roots that throw up new stems around the sides of the plant. If you see new shoots growing around the base of a mature ("parent") plant, use this simple method to divide it up to make two or three new ones. Here, we have divided a snake plant; other suitable plants that are easy to divide include cast iron plants, asparagus ferns, Boston ferns, peace lilies, and most *Goeppertia*.

WHAT YOU WILL NEED

PLANT
- Mature, healthy plant with shoots growing around the sides

OTHER MATERIALS
- Multipurpose potting soil

TOOLS
- Watering can
- Sharp, clean knife
- Plastic pots that match the size of the root balls

1 Water the plant about an hour before removing it from its plastic pot. Using your fingers, remove some of the soil from the root ball, so you can see more clearly where the stems are attached to the roots.

2 If possible, tease apart the new shoots from the parent plant, ensuring that plenty of roots remain attached to both sections.

3 If the root ball is too congested, use a sharp knife to cut it into sections, ensuring that the stems all have some roots (severing a few roots is fine).

4 Fill new pots with multipurpose potting soil. Plant the divisions in the pots, taking care not to damage the roots. Set them at the same level they were growing at in their original pot; do not bury the stems. Water, and set in a warm, bright spot out of direct sun.

PROPAGATE FROM
OFFSETS

Offsets are young plantlets (known as "pups") that grow from the parent plant. Some plants produce offsets that replace the parent when it dies after flowering; this is the case for all bromeliads (shown here), as well as some cacti and succulents. Mature spider plants, meanwhile, regularly produce offsets from long cascading stems, which can be potted up to create new plants (see opposite).

WHAT YOU WILL NEED

PLANT
- Mature, flowering bromeliad with offsets growing around the base

OTHER MATERIALS
- Hormone rooting powder
- Cactus potting soil (or a 2:1 mix of multipurpose potting soil and sand)
- Perlite

TOOLS
- Sharp, clean knife
- Soft, clean brush
- 4in (10cm) plastic pots
- Short stick for staking
- Small watering can with a rose attachment

1 Check that the offsets around the base of the plant are between one-third and one-half of the size of the parent before removing them. These will root more successfully than younger offsets.

2 Carefully remove the plant from its pot. With a sharp knife, cut off the offset close to the parent. Try not to damage the parent plant; it can be repotted if it has not died back, as it may yet go on to produce more offsets.

3 If there is a papery leaf covering the end of the offset, pull this back to reveal the base and dust with hormone rooting powder. Do not worry if the base does not yet have roots; they are not essential for success at this stage, as the powder will encourage root growth.

4 Fill a 4in (10cm) plastic pot with cactus potting soil mixed with a handful of perlite. Insert the base of the offset into the soil, taking care not to bury too much of the stem, which may rot. Water lightly to settle the soil around the offset.

5 If the offset is too heavy to stand up on its own, stake it with a short stick. Set the pot in a bright position out of direct sun, and keep the soil moist but not wet. Roots will develop after a few weeks. Repot when new shoots appear, following the advice for your bromeliad in the Plant Profiles chapter (see pp.102-05). Offsets take 2–3 years to mature and flower.

POTTING UP "SPIDER" OFFSETS

Spider plants are easy to propagate from the offsets (known as "spiders," which give the plant its name). These grow at the ends of long stems that cascade down from the parent plant.

1 Wait until your plant has produced a few small leafy offsets at the tips of the cascading stems. Look for those that are healthy and have a few sets of leaves.

2 Select an offset with a tiny root growing from the base. Fill a small plastic pot with cuttings potting soil, and set the offset into it; do not bury the offset too deeply.

3 Do not cut the offset from its parent yet. Keep the soil moist, and wait for new shoots to appear. This is a sign that the offset has made its own root system, and you can then cut it free from the parent plant.

PROPAGATE FROM SEED

Raising plants from seed is easier than you may think, but be prepared to pamper the seedlings for a couple of months while they are developing into mature plants, as any periods of drought could kill them. Annual plants (which grow, flower, and die in the same year) are good choices for beginners, and include the Persian violet, impatiens, and coleus (shown here). Buy fresh seeds every year for the best results.

WHAT YOU WILL NEED

PLANT
- Packet of houseplant seeds

OTHER MATERIALS
- Seed and cuttings potting soil
- Vermiculite

TOOLS
- Small seed tray with clear plastic lid
- Sieve, for soil (optional)
- Plant labels
- Small spoon
- Module seed tray or small plastic pots
- Watering can fitted with a rose attachment
- Larger pots
- Multipurpose potting soil

1 Almost fill a seed tray with damp seed potting soil. Press the upturned lid of the seed tray on top to create a flat surface and to remove any air gaps. Sow seeds evenly on the surface.

2 Cover the seeds with vermiculite or a very thin layer of sieved potting soil. Label, put on the lid, and set in a bright area out of direct sun; the seeds need light to germinate.

3 Keep the soil moist but not wet. Remove the lid as soon as the first leaves emerge, and leave the seedlings to grow on until they have formed 4–6 new leaves.

4 Fill a module seed tray or plastic pots with seed potting soil. Make a hole with the spoon, then use it to scoop out a seedling, keeping its roots intact. Hold it by its leaves and plant it into one of the modules.

5 Gently firm around the base of the seedling. Repeat until the whole tray is filled with seedlings, then water with a can fitted with a rose attachment. Keep the potting soil moist but not wet; overwatering may rot the seedlings.

6 Place the tray or pots of seedlings in a warm, bright area out of direct sun to grow on. Turn them every day or two so that the plants grow evenly and do not stretch toward the light and become tall and leggy.

7 When the seedlings are about 4–6in (10–15cm) tall, transplant them into larger pots of multipurpose potting soil. Nip out the stem tips to encourage bushier growth (see p.194). They will soon grow into mature plants, ready to display.

WHAT'S WRONG
WITH MY PLANT?

If your plant is not looking its best, this simple checklist may help you to determine the potential cause. Inspect the plant carefully for symptoms and try to identify the likely cause of the problem, then take appropriate action. Most issues can be fixed with just a few care adjustments, so always try the simplest remedies first.

CAUSES AND SOLUTIONS

Once you've identified the most likely cause of your plant's ailment, turn to the following pages to find the solution:

Care-based problems are usually the most likely cause of poor houseplant health. **(pp.212–13)**

Diseases can also be a potential cause; familiarize yourself with the warning signs and learn how to treat them. **(pp.214–15)**

Pests are another possibility, so watch out for them and remove them if you spot any. **(pp.216–19)**

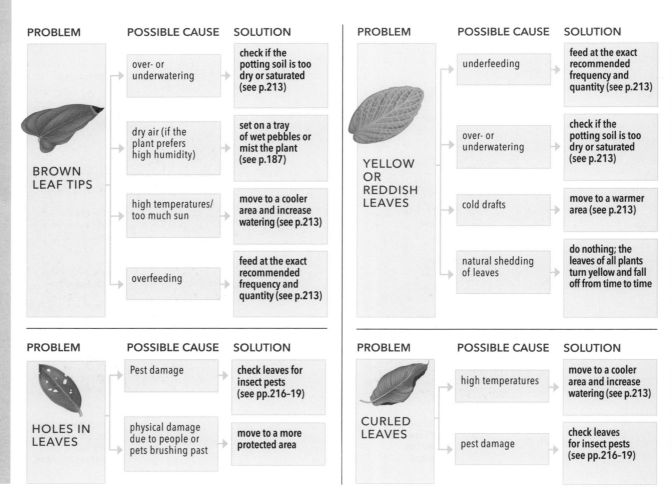

PROBLEM	POSSIBLE CAUSE	SOLUTION
BROWN LEAF TIPS	over- or underwatering	check if the potting soil is too dry or saturated (see p.213)
	dry air (if the plant prefers high humidity)	set on a tray of wet pebbles or mist the plant (see p.187)
	high temperatures/ too much sun	move to a cooler area and increase watering (see p.213)
	overfeeding	feed at the exact recommended frequency and quantity (see p.213)

PROBLEM	POSSIBLE CAUSE	SOLUTION
YELLOW OR REDDISH LEAVES	underfeeding	feed at the exact recommended frequency and quantity (see p.213)
	over- or underwatering	check if the potting soil is too dry or saturated (see p.213)
	cold drafts	move to a warmer area (see p.213)
	natural shedding of leaves	do nothing; the leaves of all plants turn yellow and fall off from time to time

PROBLEM	POSSIBLE CAUSE	SOLUTION
HOLES IN LEAVES	Pest damage	check leaves for insect pests (see pp.216–19)
	physical damage due to people or pets brushing past	move to a more protected area

PROBLEM	POSSIBLE CAUSE	SOLUTION
CURLED LEAVES	high temperatures	move to a cooler area and increase watering (see p.213)
	pest damage	check leaves for insect pests (see pp.216–19)

PROBLEM	POSSIBLE CAUSE	SOLUTION
SPOTS ON LEAVES	dark brown spots: overwatering	check the potting soil is not saturated (see p.213)
	dry patches: underwatering	water more frequently to keep the soil moist (see p.213)
	pale spots: misting with hard water	use unsoftened water to mist the plant
	disease or pest damage	check leaves for diseases and pests (see pp.214–19)

PROBLEM	POSSIBLE CAUSE	SOLUTION
SUDDEN LEAF FALL	environmental change due to repotting or new position	wait a few days; the plant should soon recover
	pest damage	inspect roots for insect pests (see pp.216–19)

PROBLEM	POSSIBLE CAUSE	SOLUTION
FLOWER BUDS FALL	dry air (if the plant prefers high humidity)	set on a tray of wet pebbles or mist the plant (see p.187)
	under- or overwatering	check if the potting soil is too dry or saturated (see p.213)
	wrong temperature	check advice and move if too hot or too cold (see p.213)
	pest damage	check buds, stems, and leaves for insect pests (see pp.216–19)

PROBLEM	POSSIBLE CAUSE	SOLUTION
WILTED LEAVES AND STEMS	over- or underwatering	check if the potting soil is too dry or saturated (see p.213)
	root-bound	repot the plant into a container one or two sizes larger so roots can absorb water more easily
	high temperatures/ too much sun	move to a cooler area and increase watering (see p.213)
	pest damage	check the leaves and roots for insect pests (see pp.216–19)

PROBLEM	POSSIBLE CAUSE	SOLUTION
FURRY GROWTH ON LEAVES AND STEMS	fungal diseases	identify the disease (pp.214–15) and treat as suggested

PROBLEM	POSSIBLE CAUSE	SOLUTION
NO FLOWERS	too little light	move into an area with more sun (see p.212)
	over- or underfeeding	feed at the exact recommended frequency and quantity (see p.213)
	dry air or soil	mist the plant if it likes high humidity and check if the potting soil is too dry (see p.213)
	pot too big	repot into a smaller pot; some plants only flower when roots are restricted

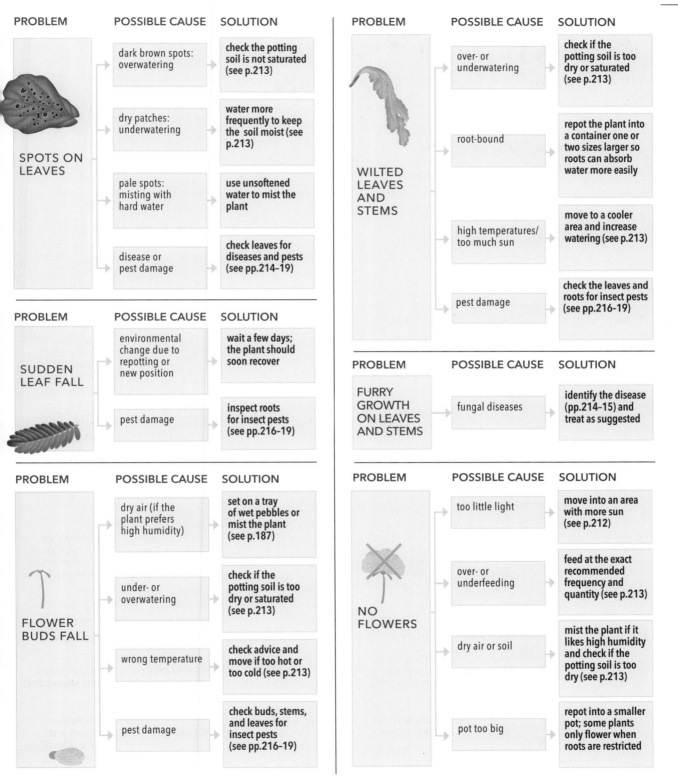

DEALING WITH
CARE-BASED PROBLEMS

Most houseplant health issues are simply the result of incorrect care, and in most cases they are easily fixed. Once you have identified the most likely cause of the problems (see pp.214–15), use this guide to find the best ways to bring it back to health.

CARE COMES FIRST

To keep your plant thriving, follow the care advice given in the Plant Profiles chapter (see pp.100–75), as well as the tips outlined here if it starts to show any signs of poor health. If problems persist a few days after you have taken action to rectify them, the cause may lie elsewhere. Return to pp.210–11 to see if a disease or pest may be the cause, then follow the suggested solutions. Remember that plants will be more resilient to attacks if they are given the right care and conditions.

Plants standing in insufficient light will become misshapen as the stems stretch toward the sun

GOLDEN RULES FOR KEEPING YOUR PLANTS HEALTHY

1 Check the light, temperature, watering, and fertilizing needs of your plants in the Plant Profiles chapter (see pp.100–75).

2 Plant in pots with drainage holes and water so that the potting soil does not become waterlogged.

3 Place your plant in the right amount of light for its needs.

4 Stand the plant in the right temperature, away from heaters, and provide good ventilation.

5 Feed a plant according to its requirements—both over- and underfeeding can be harmful.

6 Remove fallen leaves or flowers from the soil, which may rot and lead to fungal disease.

7 Check the plant every few days for signs of pests or diseases.

8 Cut out any diseased plant parts and remove any pests promptly.

INSUFFICIENT LIGHT

THE PROBLEM Standing your plant in enough light is critical to its health; too little sun can lead to tall, spindly stems and lopsided growth, yellow or pale leaves, and few or no flowers.

THE SOLUTION Check that your plant is given the light it needs in the Plant Profiles chapter (see pp.100–75). Prevent the stems reaching for the sun and growing tall and weak ("etiolated"), or lopsided, by turning the pot every few days.

TOO MUCH LIGHT

THE PROBLEM Even some sun-loving plants cannot tolerate the intense light of midsummer sun. Symptoms include brown leaf tips, brown upper leaf surfaces, and wilting.

THE SOLUTION Move your plant from a sunny window or room to an area in diffused light, or hang net curtains over windows.

TOO COLD

THE PROBLEM Cold drafts can cause the leaves to turn yellow or red and then fall off. Occasionally, leaves can also look deformed due to a drop in temperature halting normal growth.

THE SOLUTION Keep plants away from cold drafts, such as hallways, and remove them from cold windowsills, especially at night, in winter.

Move plants from cold windowsills during the winter months.

TOO WARM

THE PROBLEM High temperatures can make the soil dry out, dehydrating your plant, and may also reduce the humidity levels in the air. Symptoms can include brown leaf tips, curled leaves, wilting, falling flower buds, or no flowers.

THE SOLUTION Keep plants away from hot, direct sunlight in summer, and open windows or turn on the air conditioning to lower temperatures. Also water more frequently when temperatures rise to keep the potting soil moist (but not too wet—see right), and move plants away from heaters in winter.

UNDERWATERING

THE PROBLEM Potting soil that is too dry can lead to wilting, brown leaf tips, yellow or red leaves, curled leaves, falling flower buds, or no flowers.

SOLVE IT Plants will recover quickly after dry soil is watered, and they should perk up after a day or two. Watering from below may be the best method if soil is very dry (see p.184), but guard against overwatering.

OVERWATERING

THE PROBLEM The symptoms of underwatering (above) can also be a sign of overwatering, as the roots begin to rot due to the excess moisture, preventing them from taking up water. Overwatering can also cause fungal diseases (see pp.214–15) and spots on the foliage, caused by a condition called "edema," where water-soaked patches on the leaves rupture and turn corky.

THE SOLUTION Pour away excess water in the plant's decorative waterproof pot or tray, and repot if its root ball is in a container with no drainage holes. Then leave the plant to dry out on a draining board or tray filled with dry gravel.

Edema is caused by overwatering and results in corky patches on leaves

UNDERFEEDING

THE PROBLEM Tell-tale signs of an undernourished plant include pale leaves, yellow foliage, poor overall growth, and few or no flowers.

THE SOLUTION Feed your plants according to their care instructions in the Plant Profiles chapter (pp.100–75). Do not be tempted to overfeed, though, even if you think your plant is malnourished, as this could lead to reverse osmosis (see below), which will also harm the plant.

Pale or yellow leaves are often the first signs of nutrient deficiency

OVERFEEDING

THE PROBLEM Overfeeding can cause similar symptoms to underfeeding (above), since an excess of fertilizer can draw nutrients out of a plant's cells in a process known as "reverse osmosis." It can also cause brown leaf tips.

THE SOLUTION Flush the potting soil through with plenty of plain water; use unsoftened water if that is what your plant prefers (see the Plant Profiles chapter, pp.100–75). Make sure that the plant pot has drainage holes so excess water and nutrients can escape easily.

DEALING WITH COMMON DISEASES

Even with the best care, plants can still succumb to disease. If this happens, isolate the plant to prevent the problem from spreading, identify the ailment, then take appropriate action as soon as possible.

PREVENTION IS BETTER THAN CURE

Among the most common causes of plant diseases are overwatering, underwatering, and lack of ventilation, which allow rots and other fungi to develop, so follow the advice given on p.213 to keep yours healthy. If your plant still succumbs to disease, ventilate the room if controlling it with a spray fungicide, and disinfect pots to prevent reinfection.

FUNGAL LEAF SPOT

THE PROBLEM Dark spots with yellow edges appear on the leaves, and the foliage may then fall off.

THE SOLUTION Remove affected leaves as soon as you see them, along with any foliage that has fallen onto the soil. Provide more ventilation around the plant to prevent reinfection, and treat persistent problems with a fungicide.

POWDERY MILDEW

THE PROBLEM This disease produces a white, powdery fungus on leaves, stems, and flowers, and is often caused by lack of water and poor ventilation.

THE SOLUTION Check that your plant is not stressed due to underwatering, which increases the risk of infection. Remove affected parts as soon as you see them, and make sure the air is well ventilated. Apply a fungicide in severe cases.

DOWNY MILDEW

THE PROBLEM This fungal disease causes green, yellow, purple or brown blotches on the leaves and a moldlike growth under the foliage. The leaves can also turn yellow and fall.

THE SOLUTION Remove affected parts, and bag and throw out severely infected plants. Avoid wetting the leaves, which can increase the likelihood of mildew developing. There is no chemical cure.

DAMPING OFF

THE PROBLEM This affects seedlings, where the ventilation is poor, or seeds have been sown too thickly. Seedlings collapse and quickly die, and a white fungal growth appears on the potting soil.

THE SOLUTION As soon as the seedlings emerge, remove any lid or plastic covering so that air can circulate. There is no chemical cure.

GRAY MOLD

THE PROBLEM The first sign of this fungal disease is usually a fuzzy gray-brown mold on the plant's stems and leaves, which soon leads to their decay.

THE SOLUTION Remove affected parts as soon as you see them, and provide more ventilation around the plant. Control with a fungicide as soon as you see the mold, or the plant may die.

SOOTY MOLD

THE PROBLEM A black or dark brown fungal growth appears mainly on the leaves. It is caused by fungus growing on the sugar-rich honeydew produced by sap-sucking pests, such as aphids.

THE SOLUTION Remove the pests (see pp.216–219) if possible, and wipe off the fungus with warm water. There is no chemical cure.

STEM AND CROWN ROT

THE PROBLEM This fungal disease turns stems from brown to black around the soil line, and this discoloration can then travel up the plant to the leaves. The plant will begin to show signs of wilting and then start to decay.

THE SOLUTION Once symptoms show, it may be too late to halt the dieback of the plant. To prevent this rot, check that the potting soil is not soggy; plant in a pot with drainage holes and always tip excess water out of the outer pot or tray. There is no chemical cure.

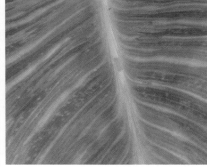

ROOT ROT

THE PROBLEM Often unnoticed until the plant wilts and will not recover after watering, this fungus is caused by prolonged drought or overwatering. The roots look dark brown or black, then rot.

THE SOLUTION Bag up and throw out affected plants, as there are no chemical cures for this rot. Prevent it from happening again by ensuring your plants' potting soil is not too wet or dry.

RUST

THE PROBLEM The rust-colored pustules caused by this fungal disease appear mainly on the undersides of leaves, which then turn yellow and die. Rust mostly affects garden plants, but can infect pelargoniums grown indoors.

THE SOLUTION Avoid overfeeding, which increases the risk of infection. Remove affected leaves as soon as you see them. There is no chemical cure.

VIRUS

THE PROBLEM Pale green or yellow spots, streaks, mosaic patterns, or rings appear on the leaves, and overall growth may be stunted or distorted. The flowers may also have white or pale streaks.

THE SOLUTION Bag up and throw out infected plants promptly to prevent spread. Do not use a plant with a suspected virus for propagation. There is no chemical cure.

DEALING WITH
COMMON PESTS

They may be small but, given the chance, many pests can quickly ruin your precious houseplants. By checking regularly for pests, you can take action to remove them before they infest your plants, which will make control more difficult.

KEEP UNWELCOME VISITORS AT BAY

Plant pests can enter your home on new houseplants that you have bought in, so when buying, always check for them on the leaves, stems, and flowers, and look for insects crawling on the soil. Open windows and doors also offer pests a route inside, but by giving your plants a health check every week, you should be able to keep most under control by simply picking them off. A few, such as spider mite, are difficult to see with the naked eye, so look out for the tell-tale symptoms and take the necessary action to keep your plants free of pests.

APHIDS

THE PROBLEM These common sap-sucking insects can grow up to ¼in (7mm) long. They cause distorted or curled leaves, stunted flower buds, and poor overall growth. Aphids also excrete a sticky honeydew, which can lead to the growth of sooty molds (see p.215).

THE SOLUTION Look for aphids on flower buds, on stems (below), and under the leaves. To remove them, wear plastic gloves and gently squeeze them, then wipe them off. For larger infestations, try a dilute soap-based solution or pesticide.

These tiny flying insects cause silvery discoloration on leaves

THRIPS

THE PROBLEM These minute, winged, sap-sucking insects are only ¹⁄₁₆in (2mm) long and difficult to see unless they are flying around. Their nymphs (juveniles) are wingless. Damage results in dull green leaves with a silvery discoloration and tiny black dots on the upper surfaces. They also cause distorted shoots and flower buds, while the flowers may have white markings and lose their color, or the buds may fail to open.

THE SOLUTION Use sticky traps to help to ensnare these tiny insects. Pesticides that control thrips are also available.

EARWIGS

THE PROBLEM These nocturnal brown insects are up to ½in (15mm) long, and have distinctive pincers on their rear ends. They eat flowers and leaves, reducing the latter to a skeleton of veins. While they are not a common houseplant pest, they may attack some of the flowering types.

THE SOLUTION Inspect your plants at night and remove any insects you find. Also check inside ornamental containers or pots nearby, where they may be hiding during the day.

Identify earwigs by their long antennae and pincers at the tail end

STEM AND BULB NEMATODES

THE PROBLEM Nematodes are not visible to the naked eye, yet they can cause severe damage, feeding on the plant's fluids and leading to distorted leaves, often with yellow blotches. The stem tips and buds may also turn black and die. Nematodes can infect bulbs, too, leading to similar symptoms in the foliage, as well as yellowish swellings or specks on the undersides of leaves.

THE SOLUTION Remove affected plant parts as soon as you see them, and buy firm, healthy-looking bulbs from reputable suppliers. There are no chemical controls.

Nematodes cannot be seen by the naked eye; look for distorted yellow leaves instead

FUNGUS GNATS

THE PROBLEM Also known as sciarid flies, these grayish-brown insects grow up to ¼in (4mm). They are a nuisance, but do not generally eat live plants; they simply fly around them and run over the potting soil in seed flats. Their larvae are white maggots with black heads, slightly larger than the adults, and feed on decaying leaves or roots, and occasionally seedlings, but rarely mature plants.

THE SOLUTION Use sticky traps to ensnare the flies, and a drench of the nematode *Steinernema feltiae* to control the larvae.

Leafhoppers cause leaves to become lightly mottled

LEAFHOPPER

THE PROBLEM These small, pale green insects are about ⅛in (3mm) long and can jump from leaf to leaf, flying short distances when disturbed. The creamy white, wingless nymphs (juveniles) and their white cast skins can be easier to spot than the adults. Both cause a pale mottling on leaf surfaces, but the damage does not seriously affect the plant.

THE SOLUTION Leave the pest uncontrolled, as it rarely causes serious symptoms.

"Check your plants weekly and, if possible, pick off any insects you find."

MEALYBUGS

THE PROBLEM These sap-sucking pests look like tiny white woodlice and cause distorted or stunted growth. You will first notice a fluffy white substance in between the leaves and stems or under the foliage—the bugs or their orange-pink eggs are hiding beneath it. They also secrete honeydew, which can lead to sooty mold (see p.215), and a few species attack the roots.

THE SOLUTION Often brought in on new plants, check for bugs before buying. Remove affected parts or apply dilute solutions of soap-based products or denatured alcohol with a brush (test a small area first to check that it will not harm the plant). Or use pheromone lures to trap the adult males and disrupt breeding. Throw out badly infested plants; pesticides rarely work.

A fluffy white substance hides mealybugs and their eggs

ROOT APHIDS

THE PROBLEM These aphids feed on plants' roots, sucking the sap from them, just like those that live above the soil. However, because they are hidden, you will notice the symptoms before the pests. Leaves will become stunted, wilt, and turn yellow as the insects destroy the roots.

THE SOLUTION If watering does not revive a wilting plant, check for root aphids in the soil. Try washing off the potting soil and aphids outside, then repot in fresh soil, as there is no chemical control.

Root aphids suck the moisture from roots, causing them to wither and die

SCALE INSECTS

THE PROBLEM Scales or shell-like bumps up to ½in (1cm) in length appear on stems or beneath the leaves. You may also spot the white, waxy eggs. These sap-sucking insects cause distorted and weak growth, and secrete sugary honeydew, which can lead to the growth of sooty molds (see p.215).

THE SOLUTION Remove affected parts, or apply dilute solutions of soap-based products or denatured alcohol with a paint brush (test a small area first to check that it will not harm the plant). Dispose of heavily infested plants.

SPIDER MITE

THE PROBLEM Also known as red spider mite, this tiny sap-sucking insect produces a mottled appearance on plant leaves. The foliage also loses its color and may then fall off; heavy infestations can eventually kill the plant.

THE SOLUTION Remove and throw out affected parts promptly; also trash severely infested plants to prevent the pest spreading. Misting plants regularly can reduce attacks, but may not eliminate the pest. You can also use a pesticide.

While spider mites are too small to see, mottled leaves signal their presence

SLUGS AND SNAILS

THE PROBLEM You will probably be familiar with these slimy mollusks, which eat holes in leaves and munch through stems. While they mostly affect outdoor plants, they can enter your home on new plants or through open windows.

THE SOLUTION You can normally see these pests on houseplants, or find them lurking in their ornamental pots. Pick them off and dispose of them.

"Some pests are too small to see easily; check the plant for symptoms of infestation instead."

"Watch out for grubs and nymphs— these can often be just as bad, if not worse, as the adult pest."

CATERPILLARS

THE PROBLEM Not many houseplants are affected by these pests; the most common indoors is the Tortrix moth caterpillar, which binds leaves together with fine webbing (below), causing them to dry up and turn brown, then fall off. Other caterpillars eat holes in the leaves, and you will see them usually lurking under the foliage.

THE SOLUTION Pick off caterpillars, or press the affected leaves together to kill the insects and pupae. For heavier infestations, use a pesticide that controls caterpillars; ventilate the room when applying it.

The root-eating grubs (right) cause more damage than the adult vine weevils

VINE WEEVILS

THE PROBLEM The adult black weevils are about ½in (9mm) long and easy to spot. They nibble leaves, making notches along the margins, but do little serious damage. The white, C-shaped, legless grubs with brown heads (about the same size as the adults) are the real problem because they eat the roots, causing plants to collapse and die.

THE SOLUTION Shake plants to dislodge the adults or trap them with sticky barriers around the outer pots. Try to catch the slow-moving weevils before they lay eggs in spring and summer. If you see the grubs, try hosing the roots outside to remove them, then repot in fresh potting soil, or apply the nematode *Steinernema kraussei* in fall.

WHITEFLY

THE PROBLEM These white, winged, sap-sucking insects are easy to see, even though they are just under ⅛in (2mm) in length. Clouds of flies rise up when disturbed, and you may also spot the white, scalelike nymphs on the undersides of leaves. Whitefly causes distorted leaves and buds, and stunted growth. Both adults and nymphs excrete honeydew, which can lead to black sooty mold (see p.215).

THE SOLUTION Hang sticky sheets near plants to trap the adults or spray the flies with a dilute soap-based solution, which prevents them from flying and disrupts breeding. Also try standing affected plants outside in summer where beneficial insects will help to control them, or use a pesticide.

INDEX

ACKNOWLEDGMENTS

Fran Bailey would like to give a big thank you to Amy Slack and Philippa Nash at DK for their encouragement and support; to Nigel Wright and Rob Streeter, whose vision and expertise really brought the projects to life; and to Katie Mitchell (@bymekatie) for her macramé expertise.

Zia Allaway would like to thank the whole team at DK for their dedication to detail in producing this book, with particular thanks to editor Amy Slack for her support with the words and her infinite patience, and to Christine Keilty, Mandy Earey, and Philippa Nash for their beautiful designs. Thanks also to photographer Rob Streeter and stylists Nigel Wright and Janice Browne of XAB Design for the stunning images, and to managing editor Stephanie Farrow for commissioning her and scrutinizing each page to ensure the quality was never compromised. And thanks to Christopher Young of the Royal Horticultural Society for his editorial input and fact checks. Last but not least, a huge thank you to her husband Brian North and son Callum Allaway North for their patience and support while she was writing this book.

DK would like to thank Julie Aylett, Kathy Sanger, Sue Unwin, and Irene Morris at Aylett Nurseries for their endless advice and assistance in sourcing plants; Jamie Song, John Bassam, and Jo for the hire of their homes; Jan Browne at XAB Design for behind-the-scenes help with coordinating photoshoots; Rosamund Cox and Emma Pinckard for editorial assistance; and Vanessa Bird for indexing.

DK would also like to thank the following for their kind permission to reproduce their photographs:
(Key: a-above; b-below/bottom; c-center; f-far; l-left; r-right; t-top)

GAP Photos: 33tc, Martin Hughes-Jones 33tr, Dianna Jazwinski 45br, Lynn Keddie 21bl, Howard Rice 36br, Friedrich Strauss 17tr, 17bl, 29tl, 29ftl, 33bl, 37bl, Visions 20br.
All other images © Dorling Kindersley
For further information see: **www.dkimages.com**

ABOUT THE AUTHORS

Fran Bailey grew up on a cut flower nursery near York, England, where her Dutch father Jacob Verhoef encouraged her love of all things horticultural. After studying at the Welsh College Of Horticulture, she moved to London to work as a freelance florist. In 2006, she opened her first flower shop, The Fresh Flower Company, in South London. In 2013, she expanded into houseplants with the opening of her shop Forest, which she runs with her daughters, and which is packed to the rafters with lush greenery.

Zia Allaway is an author, journalist, and qualified horticulturalist who has written and edited a range of gardening books for DK, including *Indoor Edible Garden*. Zia also writes a monthly column on garden design for *Homes and Gardens* magazine and is a contributor to the *Garden Design Journal*. She runs a consultancy service from her home in Hertfordshire, England, and offers practical workshops for beginners.

Christopher Young is the horticultural team leader of the Glasshouse at RHS Wisley, the Royal Horticultural Society's flagship garden in Surrey, England. He is a passionate plantsman with a particular interest in exotic plants and ferns, and is also a member of the RHS Tender Ornamental Plant Committee.

Editor Amy Slack
Designers Philippa Nash
with Mandy Earey, Lee-may Lim
Senior jacket creative Nicola Powling
Pre-production manager Sunil Sharma
DTP designer Rajdeep Singh
Producer, pre-production Robert Dunn
Senior producer Stephanie McConnell
Managing editor Stephanie Farrow
Managing art editor Christine Keilty
Art director Maxine Pedliham
Publisher Mary-Clare Jerram
Photographer Rob Streeter
Photographic art director Nigel Wright
Houseplant consultant Christopher Young
US consultants Judy Feldstein, John Tullock
US editor Kayla Dugger
US managing editor Lori Hand

First American Edition, 2018
Published in the United States by DK Publishing
345 Hudson Street, New York, New York 10014

Copyright © 2018 Dorling Kindersley Limited
DK, a Division of Penguin Random House LLC
18 19 20 21 22 10 9 8 7 6 5 4 3 2 1
001–308290–Feb/2018

A catalog record for this book is available from the Library of Congress.
ISBN 978-1-4654-6921-2

DK books are available at special discounts when purchased in bulk for sales promotions, premiums, fund-raising, or educational use. For details, contact: DK Publishing Special

Markets, 345 Hudson Street, New York, New York 10014
SpecialSales@dk.com

Printed and bound in China

A WORLD OF IDEAS:
SEE ALL THERE IS TO KNOW

www.dk.com